DISASTERS
on the
SEVERN

Drawing showing the Arkendale H *and* Wastdale H *smouldering the following morning after striking the Severn Railway Bridge. (Artist Louise Bloomfield)*

DISASTERS
on the
SEVERN

Chris Witts

TEMPUS

First published 2002

PUBLISHED IN THE UNITED KINGDOM BY:
Tempus Publishing Ltd
The Mill, Brimscombe Port
Stroud, Gloucestershire GL5 2QG
www.tempus-publishing.com

PUBLISHED IN THE UNITED STATES OF AMERICA BY:
Tempus Publishing Inc.
2 Cumberland Street
Charleston, SC 29401
www.tempuspublishing.com

British Library Cataloguing in Publication Data.
A catalogue record for this book is available from the British Library.

ISBN 0 7524 2383 5

Typesetting and origination by Tempus Publishing.
PRINTED AND BOUND IN GREAT BRITAIN.

Contents

Drawing showing Deans Way, Gloucester, flooded in 1947. (Artist Louise Bloomfield)

Acknowledgements

Carol Witts; Diana Harvey; Eva Lane; George Thompson; Gloucestershire Constabulary; Gloucestershire County Library; Gloucestershire Fire & Rescue Service; Gloucestershire Record Office; Hugh Conway Jones; Keith Smart; Louise Bloomfield; Rachel Edwards; Richard Whittington-Egan; Susan Jones; The Citizen; The Thornbury Society; Andrew Parry; Campbell McCutcheon.

Introduction

I felt compelled to write this book, although some would say on a morbid subject, as I believe the stories have to be told. It is fact that the River Severn is one of the most dangerous rivers in Britain and has claimed many lives.

I experienced first-hand knowledge of this when, as a sixteen-year-old, I got myself a job on one of the esturial tanker barges trading along the Severn. Within weeks of starting work on the Severn, I found myself involved in one of the most spoken about incidents, the Severn Bridge Disaster of 1960. During the following few years I again found myself involved in other tragic incidents.

Many years later I was fortunate enough to become skipper of one of the last remaining commercial cargo barges still working on the Severn. This was the 1990s, the river was still wild, but new rules and regulations went some way to making it a little safer environment to work in.

It would be very difficult to prove who was the first person to drown in the River Severn, but as history does show, at least one person has been killed in the river every year since records have been kept.

The legend of Sabrina relates to how the river got its name of Severn; first the Welsh name Habren which later became Hafren, translated into English became Sabren, then Sabrina and finally Severn.

There was a King of Loegria called Locrine who was to marry Gwendoline but, on seeing a beautiful young German maiden, took her hostage. He abandoned Gwendoline, who then fled to her father in a distressed state and persuaded him to frighten the King into marrying her. Although the marriage went ahead, Locrine kept his German maiden, Estrildis, as his mistress for seven years, hidden in a small chamber under the castle where he could visit her each night. Estrildis eventually became pregnant and gave birth to a daughter who she named Habren.

Left: a drawing of Sabrina   *Right: a drawing of King Locrine*

Soon after this Gwendoline's father died and Locrine then abandoned her again to put Estrildis on the throne. Gwendoline travelled down to Cornwall to seek the help of her brother, who returned to Dolforwyn with an army to confront Locrine at the castle. During the fight at Abermule the army seized both Estrildis and her daughter Habren and threw them into the River Severn where together they drowned.

Over 700 years later, the Severn once again took the life of a young mother due to the jealous rage of a husband, only this time it was 200 miles down stream from where young Sabrina met her fateful end.

Not all the fatalities have been accidental or by brutal means. Many deaths have been through suicide, which, until a few decades ago, was a chargeable offence. How easy it has been for the desperate person, intent on ending their life, to jump into the river from one of the many bridges crossing the Severn. Perhaps easy is the wrong word, for who knows what is going on in the mind of the suicidal person shortly before they commit themselves to this sad end.

There have been stories of bravery from men on the shore, watching their comrades in trouble out in the river. On the night of the Severn Bridge disaster, whilst the river was ablaze and crewmen from the stricken tanker barges fought for their lives, a few men on the shore at Purton jumped into a rowing boat and ventured out into the gloom. They put their own lives in danger to save others; sadly though, five men were to die that night.

One person who is too familiar with disasters on the Severn, is Capt. George Horace Thompson, skipper of the *Arkendale H* on that fateful night of 25 October 1960 when he was involved in the Severn Bridge disaster. He is a living legend, who worked on the tanker barges getting their cargoes through no matter what the weather. He has been involved in tragedies which would have finished most men who work on this dangerous waterway; his spirit is still strong, laughing and joking, and he now helps the community where he lives.

One element of danger that will never be eliminated is flooding. For whatever flood defences are built, the River Severn will still rise dramatically whenever there are long periods of rain. Water cannot be compressed so it has to go somewhere, that is over the top of the bank, flooding surrounding areas and causing misery to those who live on the flood plains. The bridges that presently cross the Severn are of sound construction, but as time marches on they will gradually become weaker. During 1795 the Severn experienced one of its worst floods, destroying many bridges as the river became a raging torrent washing everything away in its path.

With such a setting for disaster it would be impossible to mention every incident that has taken place on Britain's longest river, my apologies therefore, if I should have missed a tragedy of which you are personally aware. Even as this is written news has been received of three foolhardy men who ventured out onto the sandbanks at Westbury-on-Severn to try their hand at fishing for elvers. It was dark with a large tide due and the first the men knew of the approaching danger was the sound of the bore wave as it headed towards Pimlico Sands. Fortunately the men had mobile phones with them and called for help from the emergency services. On arrival the Fire Service launched their rescue boats at Broadoak and found the frightened men huddled under Garden Cliff, trapped by the rising water.

Chapter One
The First Severn Bridge Disaster

4 February 1939 – Tanker Barges Lost

War in Europe loomed close, making the Severn Corridor an important waterway in keeping Great Britain supplied with oil products. A large fleet of tanker barges owned by local companies, the Severn & Canal Carrying Co., John Harker Ltd and others, would load their tanks at Avonmouth to take it far inland to Stourport. Each barge would complete two round trips a week, or sometimes part of a third if weather and tide conditions were right. The first day was down to Avonmouth to load and back to Sharpness on the next tide to tie up in the entrance to the old dock above the High Level Bridge. Early next morning it was along the Gloucester & Sharpness Ship Canal to Gloucester, lock out into the Severn and then a long day getting to Stourport. The third day would be travelling back to Sharpness empty, ready to begin it all again the following day!

This schedule could not be kept up day after day, engines would break down, the river would flood, accidents would happen and, of course, the crews had to have some time off. But time off meant losing money, as the men were paid a bonus for each trip; 'trip money' as it was called. Sadly this was the root cause of many an accident, forcing the crews to work sometimes against their better judgement.

No wonder, then, that fifty-seven-year-old Henry Phillips groaned as he was woken at 4.00 a.m. and hastily got ready to leave his home at Purton to begin a long day on his barge, the *Severn Pioneer*. Bidding his wife a fond farewell, telling her he would be home by 9.00 p.m. that evening, he left the comfort of his warm cottage to travel the few miles to Sharpness Docks. His mate, thirty-five-year-old George Butler of Epney, was already on board, tidying and making cosy the small cabin. No engine to worry about as the *Severn Pioneer* was a dumb barge, a vessel without an engine, relying on a tow from a motor tanker barge.

The *Severn Pioneer*, together with the *Severn Carrier,* was to be towed by the *Severn Traveller*, all similar sized tanker barges. Although the *Severn Carrier* had an engine, it made economical sense for the three barges to travel together and only use one engine out of the three vessels. At 4.45 a.m. Albert Tonks, the twenty-nine-year-old skipper of the *Severn Traveller* gave orders to let go and all three craft slowly manoeuvred into Sharpness lock. Soon they were out in the Severn Estuary and as the tide turned were able to make good progress on the fast flowing ebbing water.

By the time they arrived at Avonmouth, daylight was breaking, making their life easier, and all three vessels proceeded to the large oil dock to each load their different liquid cargoes. The *Severn Pioneer* was booked to load 115 tons of petrol, as was the *Severn Traveller*, but with an extra 15 tons. Skipper of the *Severn Carrier*, thirty-one-year-old Reginald Stokes of

Gloucester, had also received his orders, to load 130 tons of gasoline. All three barges were soon loaded, thankfully, as being in an oil dock with safety in mind, all engines and heating had to be shut down and there is nothing worse than being on a steel tanker barge with no heating on a cold winters day!

By 4.30 p.m. that afternoon all crews were busy preparing to move off from their berths and proceed down to the large sea lock ready for the passage back to Sharpness. Again the *Severn Traveller* was to be the towing vessel, which meant engineer Frederick Vincent of Olveston had to keep a keen eye on the engine; any breakdown out in the estuary would give them all big problems. The *Severn Carrier* may not have been using her engine on this trip, but her engineer, Joubert Matthews, nineteen years old and living in Berkeley, still made sure it would start first time if needed. The motor tanker barges carried a crew of three men and the deckhand on the *Severn Carrier*, who was also nineteen years old, was Granville Knight, whilst the deckhand on the *Severn Traveller* was eighteen-year-old Walter Capener of Saul.

At 5.15 p.m. the outer gates of the sea lock opened and as Albert Tonks increased the revs on the *Severn Traveller* all three vessels slowly moved out into the murky waters of the Severn Estuary. There was a large spring tide running that night, which made the passage across The Shoots quite rough, the area now crossed by the Second Severn Crossing bridge, requiring cabin hatches to be secured and all crewmen to congregate in the wheelhouses.

The manila tow rope between each barge would have been paid out for most of its length, creating quite a long distance from the towing barge to the last third barge. The crew on this third barge would only have the sound of the waves lapping the vessel, not so on the *Severn Traveller*, here it would be noisy in the wheelhouse with the sound of the engine working hard below them. Having safely passed Charston Rock and then Beachley Point, the passage up through Slime Road would have been relatively calm, but no time to relax, as they still had to cross the Severn toward Sheperdine passing Narwood Rocks.

Shortly before arriving at the entrance to Sharpness Docks at 7.05 p.m., an hour before high water, skipper Albert Tonks had swung his vessel around to stem the fast flowing tide. A procedure he and his crew had done many times in the past. All vessels bound for the port of Sharpness have to make this manoeuvre due to the strength of the tide and no master is happy until they have their vessel tied up either in the basin or in the lock.

The deckhand on the *Severn Traveller*, Walter Capener, noticed after his vessel had completed the turn that the $5\frac{1}{2}$in thick tow rope had come adrift from the *Severn Carrier*. He yelled to Tonks, then began the arduous task of hauling it in, which he was doing as engineer Frederick Vincent came out of the engine room and proceeded to help get the rope back on board. Skipper Tonks had to swing his barge around again at full speed to get close to the *Severn Carrier* so that one of his crew could throw a heaving line to the other barge. Hauling hard on the heaving line which had the tow rope attached, the crew of the *Severn Carrier* quickly made it fast back onto the bollards on the bow of the barge.

As soon as the crew of the *Severn Carrier* realised that the tow rope had come adrift, they started the engine to stop them and the other tow, the *Severn Pioneer*, from being swept up past Sharpness Piers. Unfortunately the engine was not powerful enough to hold both barges against the fast flowing tide. It is dangerous to navigate above Sharpness Docks as the tidal race becomes very strong but soon all three vessels were above the piers at the dock entrance and heading towards the Severn Railway Bridge.

They were only 300 yards from the bridge when the tow rope was secure again, too late, though, for the *Severn Traveller* as she did not have enough power to make any progress against the tide. The first barge to strike the bridge was the *Severn Pioneer*, hitting it so hard that she sank almost immediately. This was quickly followed by the *Severn Carrier* hitting the bridge and turning turtle. Vincent on the *Severn Traveller* reacted quickly and as the *Severn Carrier* hit the bridge he slipped the tow rope, again too late. The *Severn Traveller* hit the bridge amidships on the starboard side, heeled over, and then righted herself. Vincent was thrown into the water, but was able to grab some life chains as he went over and was in the water for some considerable time before being able to haul himself back aboard.

In the gloom Frederick Vincent had seen the other two barges hit the bridge, but had not heard any shouts from the crews. He assumed that they had been thrown into the Severn on impact, as had happened to Walter Capener as his barge, the *Severn Traveller*, hit the bridge. He had been standing alongside Vincent on the aft end of the barge and after climbing back aboard began shouting for Capener, but got no reply.

A Purton man, Mr W.H. Tudor, was duty signalman that evening on the Severn Railway Bridge when he felt vibrations through the bridge. This, he assumed, must have been as the barges struck the columns of the bridge with such force.

Albert Tonks, on the *Severn Traveller*, tried to make headway with the barge, but found his propeller was not operating properly and was drifting with the tide above the Gloucester side of the bridge. He and Vincent dropped the anchor, but they still continued to drift until the anchor held on the sands north of Purton at the Royal Drift. He began to flash a light onto the shore for help and although they could see lights flashing back no one came out to them. As they came to rest at the Royal Drift, Frederick Vincent noticed the hull of the *Severn Pioneer* drifting down, back towards Sharpness.

Lionel Keedwell, the twenty-two-year-old son of the licensee of the Berkeley Arms Inn at Purton, said that at 8.25 p.m. someone had told him that there appeared to be a boat in difficulty about a mile above the Severn Bridge. He went onto the foreshore and saw the barges

Wreck of the Severn Traveller *on the sands near Purton.*

Lionel Keedwell (centre), son of the licensee of the Berkeley Arms Inn, at breakfast with two survivors of the disaster.

and began to hail one of them, but all he got was, 'We want a boat.' The *Severn Traveller* had gone too far with the tide so it was impossible to try and reach them as they drifted a further mile and soon sight of them was lost for an hour or so.

The next thing Lionel and his father saw was the navigation lights of the *Severn Traveller*, which seemed to be stranded with another barge drifting towards Sharpness. He hailed it but, as there was no response, presumed that none of the crew were on board, then watched the other barge, which seemed to be at anchor and hearing nothing from it did not go to her assistance. Mr Keedwell thought that everything was alright so went back into the inn to retire to bed for the night. Just before he turned in, however, he thought he would have a last look, so glanced out of his bedroom window and saw what appeared to be one of the barges. He felt there was something amiss so quickly dressed and went back out to the foreshore.

With the aid of shouts and a flashlight he was able to discover that there was someone on board and asked if they wanted to be taken off. Lionel gathered together some local men, George Cook, Ernest Robins, Melvin Robins, Harry Phillips and Jack Phillips to help him launch his boat into the river. Keedwell and two others, in the darkness and with great bravery, rowed out to the *Severn Traveller*, which by now had been on the sandbank for two hours, and found the two exhausted survivors of this tragedy on the barge. Albert Tonks had a wound to his face, but Frederick Vincent appeared to be uninjured. The barge had petrol streaming from her sides, the wheelhouse was completely smashed with the wheel broken away, the engine room was flooded and the cabin was sodden and in disorder.

The two survivors said that the rest of crewmen had been lost and that another barge had foundered a mile above them. Keedwell, with the others, rowed farther up the Severn and found the barge capsized with two bodies lying nearby. There was little they could do but collect items of value and then take Tonks and Vincent back to the shore. It was later established that the two bodies that Mr Keedwell had seen were those of Reginald Stokes and Henry Phillips. When brought ashore on the Sunday they were placed in a wooden outhouse at the inn and it was noted that a watch on one of the deceased had stopped at 7.10 p.m.

Sharpness Harbourmaster, Capt. G.T. Owen, had been alerted that the wreck of the *Severn Pioneer* was drifting back to Sharpness and at 9.35 p.m. gave instructions for the tug *Primrose* to go out into the river to assist with the emergency. Only the skipper, Frank Savage, could be mustered from the usual crew of the tug. He had to sail with a scratch crew of Oliver Powell, skipper of another local tug, the *Resolute*, his engineer Jack Pittaway, Sharpness Lock foreman Cecil Turl and lockman Christopher Bastholm. Shortly after leaving Sharpness Frank Savage saw the *Severn Pioneer*, now righted again, but low in the water, off the piers. Finding it very difficult to land a party on her, he had to follow the barge for nearly a mile before he could manoeuvre effectively alongside the vessel. Oliver Powell and Cecil Turl boarded the barge with some difficulty, as the tug had to be swung round, steaming against the ebbing tide, to let the two men jump from the bows onto the slippery deck of the *Severn Pioneer*, which was awash with oil from the cargo. Eventually they secured a rope to the barge and the Primrose began to tow her back into Sharpness Docks at 10.15 p.m.

Skipper Albert Tonks looking for survivors the following day.

Police and survivors look for bodies the day after the disaster. Left to right: Fred Vincent, Albert Tonks, Police Sergent Frank Jeynes and Police Inspector Wickham.

The capsized Severn Carrier *beached near Sharpness.*

Body of Joubert Matthews, recovered two miles from the scene of the disaster.

As daylight broke on the Sunday morning the full extent of the tragedy could be seen. The *Severn Traveller* was still held by her anchor on the sandbank half a mile north of Purton, whilst the *Severn Carrier* had moved again with the following tide and was now resting on the bank above the Severn Railway Bridge. That day Oliver Powell took his tug, the *Resolute*, out into the Severn with Capt. G.T. Owen on board. There was little they could do until the following day when they towed the *Severn Traveller* to the banks of the river above the Berkeley Arms Inn at Purton and secured her there.

News of the disaster travelled slowly and only a handful of people were there to see the stricken vessels. The two survivors, Albert Tonks and Frederick Vincent, both fit young men, walked out across the sands to the wreck of the *Severn Traveller* where they spent some time on board. They reported that petrol was still leaking out of the hull.

The people of Purton had been keeping a constant lookout for signs of bodies and aided the police in recovering that of Joubert Matthews from the river. Ten men had set out on that Sunday afternoon with only a wooden stretcher and ropes and had to struggle for some time in difficult conditions to reach his body. Placing the body of Joubert Matthews onto the makeshift stretcher, the men set off on the arduous treck back to the shore. The men at times were sinking deep into the soft mud and the stretcher had to be pulled through it with the aid of ropes. The body was placed with the other two in the outhouse at the Berkeley Arms. The police praised them for their tireless efforts and expressed their gratitude to those who proved of utmost assistance to them. Without their help and expert knowledge of the river the police would have experienced far greater difficulties.

The Inquest

The coroner, Sir Seymour Williams, at Berkeley Police Court, opened the inquest into the death of Henry Phillips, Reginald Stokes and Joubert Matthews. The court was crowded to its fullest capacity and extra accommodation was provided for the press and other people. Attending in their official capacities were Mr Leslie Farnfield of London for the Severn & Canal Carrying Co., Mr J. Hieatt of Gloucester for the Transport & General Workers Union, Mr A. Ingleden of Cardiff for the Sharpness Docks Co. and Inspector G.A. Wickham as an observer for the police, as well as relatives of Henry Philips.

Before the coroner heard any evidence Leslie Farnfield suggested that it might be advantageous to adjourn the inquest until the Board of Trade enquiry had been heard. Sir Seymour said he must find the cause of death to see if anyone was criminally liable for the accident. He recalled that at the time of the Charfield Railway Disaster he had Col. Pringle sit with him and this was of help to both sides.

Harold Phillips of Sharpness gave evidence for identifying Henry Phillips, barge master of Purton. His elder sister Aileen Smith Matthews identified Joubert Matthews of Berkeley and Albert Tonks identified Reginald Stokes of Gloucester.

As Albert Tonks began to give evidence, Sir Seymour told him that he need not give evidence if he felt something would transpire that would tend to imply he was criminally responsible for the accident. Tonks replied that he was perfectly willing to continue and proceeded to give his evidence. During his time in the witness box Tonks used matches to illustrate to Sir Seymour the procedure in securing the barge and the position when the collision occurred. He did agree that the primary cause of the trouble was the tow rope becoming disengaged from the *Severn Carrier*. The accident would not have happened if the rope had not separated from the barge and it was not the duty of the crew of the *Severn Traveller* to make fast the rope of the barge being towed.

He agreed with Mr Hieatt that he had obtained his position of master of the barge by promotion in the ordinary way. He said that none of the barge masters had a Masters Certificate or any form of certificate. As is still the case today with commercial barges operating on the Severn above Gloucester. Traditionally, the skipper of a barge would recommend to the company that his mate was ready to take the position of master should a vacancy occur. Certainly no exams were ever taken, all expertise was down to local knowledge.

Before adjourning the inquest until a later date, Sir Seymour Williams said that no living man could say why the rope came off the bollards on the *Severn Carrier*, but that there had been no error in navigation by the *Severn Traveller*.

Severn Pioneer, *photographed after it had been brought into Sharpness Docks*

Tanker Barges

Severn Traveller
Motor Tanker Barge, built 1935, Official Number 163859.
Built By: Charles Hill, Bristol. 130 grt, $88\frac{1}{4}$ft long, $18\frac{1}{2}$ft wide, 7ft depth.
1948: Sold to John Harker Ltd.
1957: Sold and converted to passenger vessel.
Still working on the River Severn at Worcester.

Severn Carrier
Motor Tanker Barge, built 1933, Official Number 160019.
Built By: Charles Hill, Bristol, 140 grt, 89ft long, $19\frac{1}{2}$ft wide, $7\frac{1}{3}$ft depth.
1948: Sold to John Harker Ltd.
1957: Sold to unknown buyers.

Severn Pioneer
No construction detail
Dumb Tanker Barge

A salvage vessel attempts to right the Severn Carrier *in Sharpness basin.*

Tanker Crews

Severn Traveller

Skipper: Albert Tonks (29), 18 Great Western Road, Gloucester. Saved.

Engineer: Frederick Vincent, Zion Cottage, Olveston. Saved.

Deckhand: Walter Capener (18), Saul, single man. He had been with the company for twelve months. Prior to that he had worked on the transatlantic ships, *Boston City* and *Toronto City*. He was about to embark on the *Gloucester City* when he was offered the 3rd hand's job on the tanker barge.

Severn Carrier

Skipper: Reginald Stokes (31), 91 High Street, Gloucester. A married man with four children.

Engineer: Joubert Matthews (19), Berkeley, single man. He had worked for the company since leaving school.

Deckhand: Granville Knight (19), Saul, single man. He had only left the RMS *Queen Mary* three weeks previously to join the company.

Severn Pioneer

Skipper: Henry Phillips (57), Purton. A married man with two children.

Mate: George Butler (35), a single man who had been with the company for twelve months. He was a fine swimmer and often swam in the Severn.

Chapter Two

The Second Severn Bridge Disaster

25 October 1960 – Severn Bridge Disaster

The shrill ring of the alarm clock quickly brought the young sixteen-year-old lad to his senses. 4.00 a.m., an unearthly hour to be getting up, but his tanker barge would be sailing from Monk Meadow Dock, Gloucester in an hour's time. No time for breakfast, just a quick wash before pedalling furiously on his bike the four miles from his home in Longlevens to the docks.

Chris Witts, deckhand on the *Wyesdale H*, saw that the engineer was already aboard with engine started and kettle boiling away on the galley stove. That was the most important job for any deckhand in the John Harker fleet, making tea; as long as the skipper had his mug of tea in the wheelhouse he was happy. Yet this day, Tuesday 25 October 1960, was not a happy day for the crew of the *Wyesdale H*, in fact no day was pleasant, for this was a tanker barge with an unhappy crew.

This estuarial tanker barge was part of a large fleet of vessels, owned by John Harker Ltd of Knottingley in Yorkshire, that carried oil products from as far as Swansea, to Worcester, in their larger craft. The smaller tanker barges ran from Avonmouth to Stourport. The company had been trading on the Yorkshire waterways since the nineteenth century, then expanded to trade on other British rivers, the Severn included, where they arrived in the late 1920s. Eventually they would have a large shipyard at Knottingley, where they built not only barges for their own fleet but vessels of all types for other customers, even a submarine during the Second World War. During the 1950s they began to build large tanker barges for the Severn area, carrying a cargo of 350 tons of oil and operating to all ports of the Bristol Channel, and inland as far as Worcester.

The *Wyesdale H* was unhappy because the crew didn't work well together. She had an old Yorkshireman for the skipper, a small dour chap, always seen wearing his trilby, not saying a lot to anyone. The mate, a young Gloucester man who, like the deckhand, just wanted a quiet life, did not say much either. Then there was the engineer, noisy, brash and certainly liked the sound of his voice. He would tell the mate and deckhand what to do which would upset the skipper, an argument would start and the two men would end up fighting on deck! Finally, there was the deckhand. As was normal in the Harker fleet, the fourth hand would be a young lad, told to keep quiet, only speak when spoken to and if he did something wrong, then he could expect a clip around the ear. For the deckhand on the *Wyesdale H* this was only his second week working on the vessel, in fact it was only his second month with the company. He had spent his first month on the Shell Steelmaker, a modern tanker barge with a five-man crew, on charter to Harker's and operating in the same area.

The Arkendale H *as a dumb tanker barge before the conversion to power in 1948. Shown here being towed, loaded, in the Severn Estuary.*

Arkendale H *proceeding empty across Gloucester Docks having delivered a cargo of black oil to Worcester.*

Arkendale H *proceeding empty down the Severn Estuary to Swansea.*

Above and below: Arkendale H *arrived at Swansea. Waiting for tide before locking in to load at the Queen's Dock.*

The Wastdale H *leaving Avonmouth Lock loaded bound for Sharpness.*

The *Wyesdale H* may have been unhappy to work on, but the vessel had superb accommodation: a cabin each for the four-man crew; a mess room and a galley and toilet/washing facilities, warm and cosy, located at the stern end of the barge and built around the large engine room. She was part of the famous 'Dale' fleet. In 1937 the company began naming all their vessels after the Yorkshire dales, with the suffix H, and for every 'Dale' vessel there was always a twin, the *Wyesdale H* being no exception, hers being the *Wastdale H*. Both barges were large, but with a low bow so they could only trade as far as Avonmouth; it was too dangerous to go on down to Swansea, especially in the winter with the rough seas experienced farther down the Bristol Channel.

Shortly after the skipper and mate arrived on board, the crew of both the *Wyesdale H* and *Wastdale H* let go their mooring ropes in darkness at Monk Meadow Dock, to begin the three-hour trip down the sixteen-mile Gloucester & Sharpness Ship Canal to Sharpness. There was a short wait there before being called into the sea lock along with numerous other craft, some bound for Swansea, others for Avonmouth, vessels of all types; tugs with lighters, motor barges with general cargo and even a Dutch coaster bound back to the continent.

It was still early morning as all the craft locked out of Sharpness and made their way down the estuary, the sun having risen quite high and bringing a magical look to the Severn. In the autumn sunshine the estuary looks at her best, the colours of the trees seen in the distance on the slopes of hills both sides of the river sparkle like jewels on a crown. Dazzling streaks of light move on the water as the tide recedes, helping barges on their way to Avonmouth.

Meanwhile, at Swansea, craft bound for Sharpness were commencing their slow journey up the Bristol Channel, among them the *Southdale H* and *Arkendale H*, tanker barges also owned by John Harker Ltd. The *Arkendale H* was carrying a cargo of 296 metric tons of Britoleum (black oil), heavy oil that has to have heating coils running through the tanks to keep the oil in liquid form. This tanker barge was bound for Worcester and carried a crew of four men. There was no deckhand though, as there was an extra engineer due to the fact that the barge was fitted with a boiler for the heating coils, requiring two men in the engine room. Another tanker barge leaving Swansea on that morning tide was the *Shell Traveller*, bound for Gloucester with a cargo of 400 metric tons of petrol, crewed by five John Harker men; skipper, mate, engineer and two deckhands. It would have been a pleasant day to come up the Bristol Channel, with clear blue skies, a warm sun and no wind, very different to winter days when a strong gale is blowing, tossing the barges around like corks in a bath.

On arrival at Avonmouth various types of craft, cargo barges, tugs with lighters and the many tanker barges, would lock up into this vast port. The docks would be full of large freighters from all parts of the world, with cranes continually dipping and rising, transferring cargo from ship to shore. The *Wastdale H* and *Wyesdale H* turned to port, heading out of the lock towards the far end of the oil dock, past the large mechanised oil boom, where they were to be loaded. Three hours later, all loaded, it was now time to catch up on some sleep while waiting for the evening tide to take them back to Sharpness.

First lock out of Avonmouth was about 7.15 p.m. so shortly before this time loaded craft mill around the lock entrance jostling for a good position to be first away. It was dark and there was an eerie feel about the docks that night. The air was still, there was very little noise and experienced river men were commenting on how uneasy they felt about the trip upriver. A crewman from a barge that was not sailing that night had been offered a trip back to Sharpness so that he could spend some time with his family. He declined as he had a gut feeling that all was not well and there could be trouble ahead. Wise man!

As always many small craft were in that first lock out of Avonmouth and, as the many types of vessels sped out into the mouth of the Severn Estuary, they could see lights from the tanker barges which had come up from Swansea on the afternoon tide slightly ahead of them. Thirteen vessels proceeded up the estuary that evening, including the tug *Robert A* with three lighters laden with logs bound for Lydney. Visibility was about two to three miles so the crews went down into their warm cabins, leaving the masters of each barge alone in the wheelhouse to steer the barges on their course to Sharpness.

Although visibility had not been perfect coming up the estuary towards Sharpness, it remained fairly clear until they arrived at the swinging light close to Berkeley Power Station, then they were surrounded by dense fog. This area has always been known for its thick fogs, caused by the low-lying land on the foreshore being warmed by the autumn sunshine then cooled by the evening air blowing over the land.

At about 9.30 p.m. the bell in the accommodation of the *Wyesdale H* began to ring, summoning the deckhand on deck to see what the skipper wanted. The lad was shocked to see that they were surrounded by a thick fog, so bad that it was impossible to see the bow from inside the wheelhouse. Orders were given to summon the mate and to get on the bow and listen for the foghorn at Sharpness. For the lad it was his first time out in the river in fog and, having listened to the tales of those river men only a few hours previously, he would not be sorry to see the safety of Sharpness Docks. Suddenly out of the fog appeared the bow of the *Wastdale H* with mate and lad also listening for the foghorn. The two lads on each barge exchanged words and then were lost again in the fog.

The tide was flowing up the river at about 5 knots that night and increasing in speed above Sharpness, giving each skipper the added problem of holding their barges safely in a position ready to make the difficult manoeuvre between the piers and into the lock. As the tide could be more powerful than the engines on the barges it required the skippers to turn their barges around to stem the tide whilst passing Berkeley Power Station, then carefully dropping back slowly towards Sharpness whilst still punching the tide, barely holding themselves against the strong flowing current.

The *Arkendale H* was 40.3m long and 6.7m wide and had been built as a dumb tanker barge in 1937 and converted to a motor tanker barge in 1948. Skippered by George Thompson (35), he had swung his barge around earlier at Berkeley Power Station to stem the tide and as he did so he noticed the fog coming across the river from the foreshore. Before being completely enveloped in the fog he had managed to reach Sharpness Piers and as well as sounding his horn, kept a listen out for the fog siren located on the end of one of the piers. Pushing ahead against the tide George Thompson could again hear the fog siren on his port bow but, as he began to make the turn to go between the piers, he saw the tug *Addie* with a string of barges in tow going across his bows. To avoid a collision he took power off the engine of the *Arkendale H*, which unfortunately caused the barge to drift past the piers again. Finding himself in comparatively slack water above the old harbour entrance he began to line his vessel up to proceed back down the river to the harbour entrance.

Shortly after the *Arkendale H* had passed Sharpness Piers, the tanker barge *Shell Traveller* entered the harbour, whereupon the assistant Harbourmaster shouted to Tommy Carter, master of the tanker barge, informing him that there was a vessel some way up the river. Tommy Carter realised that it could be the *Arkendale H* and tried to make contact by the radiotelephone, but received no reply. He then called the *Southdale H* and asked her master to call the *Arkendale H*, but he also failed to get a reply.

Joey Lane, skipper of the tug *Addie*, had picked up the sound of the Sharpness fog siren and using that as his bearing speedily got the tug and tow between the piers and into the lock. He hadn't realised though, that his tug and the *Arkendale H* had been on a converging course, the fog so thick that he could only find his way between the piers by taking a sound bearing from the fog siren.

With full power on his eight-cylinder Gleniffer engine, George Thompson lined up the *Arkendale H* to begin the crawl against the tide back to the harbour entrance. At best his vessel would only manage 7 knots and that was with the propeller in peak condition. Upstream of Gloucester, the Severn took its toll on barges continually rubbing the bed of the river, damaging the propellers whilst striking submerged debris. As he turned his wheel to alter course Thompson's mate, Percy Simmonds (34), shouted out that there was another vessel fine on their port bow. It was the *Wastdale H* with master James Dew (42), who was a relief skipper on the barge, only on his second trip.

The *Wastdale H* had been built at Sharpness nine years earlier in 1951 with a length of 39.9m and 6.4m wide and with a good propeller could obtain a maximum of 7 knots when loaded. Unknown to him, James Dew had followed the same course as the *Arkendale H* and got himself too close to the bank below Sharpness Piers. Unfortunately the stern of the *Wastdale H* touched the bank and held on the mud and had to take assistance from another vessel to be pulled off. Dew too passed the harbour entrance, losing the sound of the foghorn, with his vessel being taken with the current towards the old and disused dock entrance. George Thompson was still sounding his whistle and James Dew, on hearing this, could then pick out the mast lights of the *Arkendale H*. As the mate of the *Arkendale H* shouted that there was another vessel on their port bow Thompson recognised her as the *Wastdale H* and knew that Dew was still a stranger to the river. He shouted to him, 'Do you know where you are?' Without waiting for a reply he told Dew that they were abreast of the Old Dock entrance. Slowly both vessels came together and unknown to both skippers, who were aft in their wheelhouses, a crew member on the bow had tied both barges together.

James Dew gave his four-cylinder Ruston 4 engine full power and the wheel hard to starboard to try to push the *Arkendale H* away, whilst George Thompson gave his vessel port wheel to keep the barge heading into the tide. With both men not knowing that their barges had been tied together at the bow they could not hold the vessels against the tide and soon they were out of control as they were taken out into the fast-flowing current. The barges, still locked together, travelled sideways up the river heading towards the Severn Railway Bridge.

All eight crew of both vessels were on deck, the two skippers in the wheelhouses, some on the bow and the remainder stood at the stern. They had four minutes of fear as both barges fought to break apart; George Thompson put his wheel hard to starboard with an endeavour to swing the barge around and stem the tide again. Meanwhile skipper of the *Wastdale H*, James Dew, put his engines full astern to hopefully pull away from the *Arkendale H*. Too late, for suddenly the Severn Railway Bridge was looming up on his port side and the barge struck column number seventeen with the bluff of the port bow. The bridge shook with the impact as the barges lay against the column, then the *Wastdale H* turned over onto her port side with the force of the tide pushing the *Arkendale H* on top of the sinking barge. George Thompson was coming out of the wheelhouse as two spans of the bridge dropped from 21m onto the two barges, the impact throwing him against the bulkhead and he was temporary knocked unconscious. James Dew was thrown into the water from his barge with the impact, but managed to cling to a rail and climb back aboard.

At 10.16 p.m. signalman Donald Dobbs gave the all-clear for the Lydney-to-Stoke train to cross the Severn Railway Bridge. After the train had passed over the bridge another railway

Railway lines from the damaged Severn Railway Bridge lie across the sand and the two tanker barges.

A view of the gap in the Severn Railway Bridge after two spans were knocked down following the collision by the two tanker barges.

worker, Mr T.C. Francis, left the Severn Bridge station signal box at 10.30 p.m. to walk down to the bridge and could see the lights of Sharpness and hear the roar of the tide as it swept up through the columns of the bridge. Suddenly he saw a sheet of red flame shoot up into the sky from beneath the bridge, followed by an explosion, then silence. He ran onto the bridge and was horrified to see the two tankers burning below with flames almost reaching the decking of the bridge and, without hesitation, he ran back to the signal box to telephone the emergency services. On returning to the bridge he could see the gaping hole where the two spans had been, with the gas main and electric cable ripped away. The barges were still burning fiercely and by this time the tide had carried both craft, together with two spans of the bridge collapsed across them, farther upstream of the bridge where they were grounded on a sandbank.

George Thompson quickly regained consciousness and made his way aft to the stern of the *Arkendale H* where he could see two of his crewmen standing in the well deck. He knew that both men could not swim so gave them each a life ring and stood between them, then he took their hands and told them to jump into the river with him. The river was ablaze with petrol from the ruptured cargo tanks of the *Wastdale H* while the *Arkendale H* was also on fire and sinking. Thompson jumped and, as he hit the water, looked back only to see that both crewmen had stayed behind. He had no choice but to swim clear of the wreckage away from the burning fuel oil.

James Dew, clinging to the rail, managed to pull himself up and clamber onto the *Arkendale H,* where he realised that her engines were still running ahead, turning the propeller which by now was out of the water. He tried to make his way to the wheelhouse to stop the propeller, but as he got there it burst into flames. As he made his way to the stern end he could see that the remaining two crewmen had inflated a life raft, but it had drifted away as it was thrown into the water. Dew told the men that they must get off the barge and led them down the deck where they were able to walk into the water.

Engineer, Jack Cooper (43), was swept by the current around to the stern of the barge where he sustained injuries to his back from the revolving propeller of the *Arkendale H.* Jack, although in pain, could not face the prospect of being burnt to death by the sea of fire from the petrol around him. He decided it would be best to give up the struggle of staying afloat

Daybreak the day following the collision with the Severn Railway Bridge. The Arkendale H *and* Wastdale H *lie together, smouldering in the mud of the Severn Estuary off Sharpness.*

The smouldering Arkendale H *lying in the mud of the Severn Estuary the following day.*

and to sink beneath the burning oil. As he was sinking he began to have thoughts of his family at home and realised how much they would miss him, so fought his way back to the surface. The tide, now ebbing, had taken him to Wellhouse Bay, a little way below the bridge on the Lydney side, to leave him stranded, but still alive, on a sandbank.

The sound of the explosion could be heard by the crew members of the *Wyesdale H*, still punching against the incoming tide trying to locate Sharpness piers in the thick fog. They could see an orange glow in the distance, in the direction of the bridge, and their first thoughts were that workmen had had an accident with machinery or gas cylinders on the bridge. The cargo of petrol that had escaped from the ruptured tanks of the *Wastdale H* had ignited both vessels and the Severn. Fortunately, the current was taking the fire upstream, away from the numerous other craft still waiting entry to Sharpness further downstream from the railway bridge. The heat from the severe fire was so intense that it cleared the fog, thus assisting the remaining vessels still out in the river to make a safe entry into the lock at Sharpness. Although bound for Lydney, Robert Young of Bristol, skipper of the tug *Robert A*, decided to make the safer entry into Sharpness, with the river ablaze and the tide still flowing he thought it too dangerous to go back across the river. Tommy Carter, master of the *Shell Traveller*, who had been patiently waiting in the lock to be levelled up for entry into Sharpness Docks, asked the lock foreman to fill the lock quickly so that he could get his vessel tied up in the docks and then possibly assist with rescuing crew members of the two stricken vessels.

At the time of the accident the Chief Fire Officer of Gloucestershire Fire Service, together with one of his Divisional Officers and a Home Office Inspector, had been travelling from

Lydney on the A48 road towards Gloucester when they saw the glow from the explosion in the direction of the River Severn. Chief Officer Payne radioed his control at Cheltenham and was told that no call had been received regarding the explosion and on hearing this they decided to drive down to the Severn Bridge Station. They were horrified to see that the river was ablaze as far as the eye could see, for at least a mile upstream of the bridge and all across the river, which is three quarters of a mile wide at this point. Fire Service control was informed of what he saw and they confirmed that other calls were now coming in from members of the public. Berkeley Police confirmed that they had received a call stating that a petrol tanker barge was ablaze on the Sharpness Canal. With the confusing locations being given to the emergency services regarding the fire, the Fire Service dispatched fire engines from both sides of the river. The Chief Fire Officer had the agonising forty-mile drive via Gloucester to reach Sharpness before he could take charge of operations.

Extensive damage from the collision and the fire is shown in this photograph. Note the railway lines lying across the barges.

More detail showing the extensive damage from the collision and the fire.

Upon jumping from the stern of the *Arkendale H*, George Thompson found himself in thick black oil. The river was on fire, spreading out behind him as he swam away from the barges. Swimming as close to the fire as he dared, he could see that the *Arkendale H* was going down by the bow, exposing the still revolving propeller. The *Wastdale H* was one mass of flames with both barges straddled by the two spans and railway lines of the bridge, but still afloat and drifting slowly with the tide. George swam with the current, which was taking him upstream towards Gloucester, still fully clothed accept for his shoes, covered in the thick, heavy crude oil from the cargo his barge had been carrying. He was hollering all the time and once heard someone else shouting for help, 'Is that you Bob?', he cried, but got no response.

The current had taken George three miles upstream before he was able to reach the banks of the Severn on the Lydney side. Still yelling, he pulled himself out of the water, but soon became very cold so dropped himself back into the river and lay submerged under the water

Firemen from Gloucestershire Fire Service inspect the tanker barges the day following the collision.

to help keep warm. A farmer had heard all the commotion from the explosion, together with the shouts for help, and went down to the river bank to investigate, whereby he came across George Thompson huddled in the water, still hollering. The farmer took George back to his farmhouse at Poulton Court, where his wife insisted he come inside and sit by the warm fire, although he was covered in dirty black oil. An ambulance arrived at the house to take George to hospital and told him that another survivor had been picked up further downstream near to Lydney.

James Dew, like George Thompson, swam away from the wrecked tanker barges and after a long time in the river reached shore on the Lydney side above the bridge. Basil Freeman, who lived near the bridge, had gone down to the shore and heard shouting from someone in the water. He shone his torch, shouted encouragement, but realised the man was being carried by the current away from him. He scrambled across mud and rocks for half a mile before he

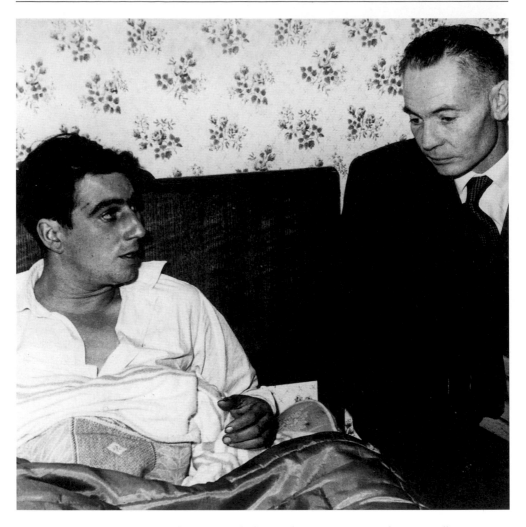

Arkendale H *skipper, George Thompson, in bed at his home in Matson, Gloucester, talking to Davy Jones, who had only recently lost his leg in an accident on another John Harker tanker, the* Southdale H.

was able to pull the man out of the cold water. Wearing his life jacket and also covered in black oil, James Dew was taken to a local inn to await the ambulance, the same one that was carrying the other survivor, George Thompson. Both men were then taken to Lydney Hospital.

From Lydney to Blakeney the word soon spread that there had been an accident on the River Severn above Sharpness and it wasn't long before crowds thronged the banks, horrified at the sight of the flames relentlessly spreading over the river. Police Sergeant Roy Cottle of Blakeney said the cries of help heard that night reminded him 'of the terrible cries heard when on convoy duty during the Second World War after a ship had gone down.' Police and others carried out an exhaustive search of the river on the Lydney side until 3.00 a.m. when they realised the tide would have carried any survivors away from them. The police also organised search parties with boats from villages above Lydney.

Tommy Carter, having safely tied up his vessel, the *Shell Traveller*, in Sharpness Docks, together with his crew, ran to the end of the piers where they could hear shouting coming from upstream of the dock entrance. He saw a small rowing boat lying on the shore and with the help of others had it loaded onto a lorry and taken to Purton, a village situated at the end of the Gloucester & Sharpness Canal. Local inhabitants and firemen took the boat from the lorry and carried it across the marshy land to the water's edge. Tommy Carter was accompanied by a carpenter from Berkeley Power Station, Charles Henderson, out onto the river to look for survivors. These were brave men who, at great risk to themselves, rowed the boat close to the flames and at one stage had to zigzag across to the Lydney side to escape from the fire. They could hear shouts for help, sometimes quite close, other times appearing to drift farther away. After some time they found Jack Cooper, engineer on the *Arkendale H*, who was exhausted and still wearing his life buoy, as well as suffering great pain from the gash in his back. He was landed on the Lydney side of the Severn and taken to the local hospital.

The Fire Service was faced with numerous problems, the first being that although they could see the burning vessels, it was proving impossible to get to them. Appliances had been deployed both sides of the Severn and with the aid of their radios they were able to be kept informed of any plan of action. On the advice of the Sharpness Harbourmaster it was decided that no appliance or firefighter would be sent out to the fire that night; it was considered, due to the hazardous nature of the tides, to be too dangerous a risk to mens' lives. A fireboat was stationed at Sharpness, but was only suitable to be used in the dock or on the canal, quite unsuitable for use on the river, especially in the conditions that night. Fire hose was laid out at both Sharpness Docks and Lydney Harbour in case the fire should spread from the river to property on the shore at either location.

A policeman looking at the two tanker barges lying in the mud of the Severn Estuary the day following the collision.

Firemen from Gloucestershire Fire Service inspect both tanker barges the day following the collision. Chief Officer Payne is shown centre of the above picture.

Firemen from Gloucestershire Fire Service inspect both tanker barges the day following the collision.

A fireman empties his boot of Severn water.

People on both sides of the river were, by this time, wandering down to the foreshore to witness the terrible tragedy. Many thought the gas pipeline across the bridge had fractured and caught fire. In fact, due to the prompt action of an employee at the Sharpness gasholder, the supply had been shut off before the escaping gas could ignite. Various impressions of what happened that night began to emerge later, as so many did not really know what was going on out in the river at the time. A young lady working on the Merchant Navy Training Ship *Vindicatrix* at Sharpness has a lasting memory of the strong smell of petrol fumes wafting over the estuary.

At 5.00 next morning vessels began leaving Sharpness Docks for the three-hour trip up the Gloucester & Sharpness Canal to Gloucester. As they passed beneath the Severn Railway Bridge on the canal between Sharpness and Purton they could see the two tanker barges out in the river still smouldering, reminding all crews of the terrible accident the night before.

Firemen from Gloucestershire Fire Service inspect the stern end of both tanker barges the day following the collision.

The ex-Aust to Beachley ferry, Severn King, *lying in the mud at low water assisting with the demolition of the Severn Railway Bridge*

REPORT OF FIRE No. K433 (7th Revision—3rd Impression)

GLOUCESTERSHIRE　　　　*Fire Brigade/Fire service*　　| Call No. |

Date and Day of Call 25th October 1960 Tuesday

~~Additional particulars to follow on form K434~~

No additional particulars to follow.*

Division, etc.　　South

Station A1.,C1.,C5.,B1.,C6.

Glos. R.D.C.

For Counties (E. & W.) only—County District (i.e., Non-County Borough, U.D.C. or R.D.C.)

~~For Scotland and N. Ireland—Administrative Area in which Fire occurred~~

1. Address of Fire　River Severn between Sharpness and Purton.	4. Method of Calling: (a) W.F.B. (b) F.B.　Exchange Telephone
2. Name(s) of Occupier(s)　　John Harker Ltd., Gloucester.	5. Discovered by　Residents on river bank.
	6. Weather　Thick fog in patches.
	7. Road condition　Wet.
	8. Wind　Light.
3. Trade(s) or Business(es) carried on: Ship Owners.	9. Time of Discovery　2235
	10. Time to Call to W.F.B.　2310
	11. Time of Arrival of W.F.B.　2325
	12. Time of Call to F.B.　2240
	13. Time of Arrival of F.B.　2259
Where fire started:　MV. WASTDALE H	14. Time under control　1007 26.10.60
	15. When last F.B. Appliance returned to Station (a) Date　26·10·60 (b) Time　1042
Where fire spread to:　MV. ARKENDALE H	16. Risk Category　D

1. **SUPPOSED CAUSE:** Two vessels collided and collided with buttress of railroad bridge. Cargo of spirit exploded on impact and set fire to cargo of oil.

2. **PARTICULARS OF PROPERTY INVOLVED:** Type No.　　Approximate date of building construction or manufacture

DESCRIPTION:

　(a) MV. WASTDALE H. G.R.T. 229.33　N.R.T. 232.49　(Petroleum spirit).

　(b) MV. ARKENDALE H. G.R.T. 229.18　N.R.T. 112.03　(Crude oil).

3. **PARTICULARS OF CONTENTS:**

4. **EXTENT OF FIRE**

　(i) Fires in Buildings.

CONFINED TO { room of origin / floor of origin / building of origin / roof or roof space

EXTENDED TO { adjoining buildings / †separate buildings / other hazards

　(ii) Fires other than those in buildings. Yes

CONFINED to hazard in which fire started

EXTENDED TO { †buildings / other hazards

5. **DESCRIPTION OF DAMAGE:** 350 tons of motor spirit and 350 tons of fuel oil destroyed by fire. Both vessels severely damaged by impact, explosion and fire. British Railways high level bridge, 2 spans totalling approximately 350ft. and 1 buttress severely damaged by impact, explosion and collapse.

6. **DEVELOPMENT OF FIRE:** Assisted by combustible ~~floor, wall, ceiling, roof lining~~*

7. **SPRINKLERS:**

　(i) ~~*Hand operated system installed~~ ~~*Automatic system installed~~ *Not installed

{ In room or section

(ii) *Failed to operate because

　(iii) Operated,　　heads being actuated, and (a) *Controlled fire. (b) *Extinguished fire.

　(c) *Did not control fire because

*Delete as necessary.　　　†See separate form(s) K.433 marked

Copy of the official Fire Report of the Severn Bridge Disaster.

8. FIRE PROTECTION APPLIANCES OR DEVICES OTHER THAN SPRINKLERS OR PORTABLE HAND OPERATED APPLIANCES:

....

9. METHOD OF EXTINGUISHING THE FIRE:
    (i) If tackled before the arrival of F.B. give details (including methods used by Works Fire Brigade):

....

    (ii) Method used by F.B.:
          Incident not accessible to Fire Service appliances.
          Precautionary measures taken on both banks of river in anticipation of
          burning oil drifting ashore.

    (iii) If immediate water supply was inadequate, give reason and details of any relay brought into operation:

....

Rescues, Escapes

Name(s)	Sex	Age (years)	Method of rescue or escape	Person effecting rescue
James Dew	M	42	Lifebelt. Walked out of	River
George H. Thompson	M	33	" " " "	"
George Cooper	M	43	Rescued by boat	Boatmen from Berkeley.

Casualties — Other than those requiring First-Aid treatment only   †For F.B. personnel add (F.B.) after name

†Name(s)	Sex	Age (years)	Address(es)	Nature of injury	If injuries prove fatal, cause of death
Malcolm Hart	M	17	Gloucester		Dead
Percy Simmonds	M	32	Gloucester		"
Albert A. Bullock	M	40	Gloucester		"
Robert J. Niblett	M	25	Hardwicke		"
Herbert J. Dudfield	M	46	Corse		"

1. F.B. APPLIANCES:
    (Give Fire Brigade (name suitably abbreviated), Division (if applicable,) and Station (number or name suitably abbreviated) from which the appliances attended, followed by the total number of appliances in brackets, e.g., "L.C.C. B. 26 (2)." Relief appliances are not to be included.)

    P.E. .... W.R.T. A1.(1),C1.(2),C5.(1),B1.(1)

    PUMPS ....
                               T/L. (Mech.) ....
                               T/L. (60' H/O.) ....
    Give particulars of other F.B. appliances:
          Foam Tender C6.(1)

2. APPLIANCES OTHER THAN F.B.   Fire Boat, British Waterways, Sharpness.

3. F.B. PERSONNEL above rank of Station Officer† attending before receipt of "stop" message (staff, visiting and relief officers need not be shown). †Note—When the officer in charge of the fire is of Station Officer rank, or below, his name should be entered.

Designation of Station or Headquarters to which attached	Rank	Name
Fire Service H.Q.	Chief Officer	Payne

4. TOTAL NO. OF PERSONNEL ATTENDING: (a) Whole-time:— 14   (b) Part-time:— 32

Signature ....
                                  Officer in charge of Station

Date ....

J9 Dd.823737 500m GP 10/71

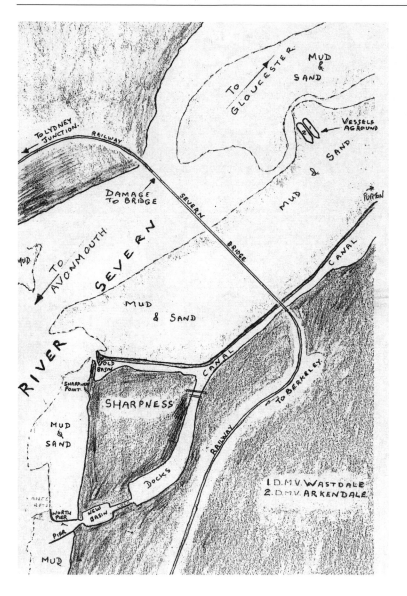

Only three men survived the accident; two skippers and an engineer. Five men were deemed to have been killed in the explosion: from the *Arkendale H*, mate Percy Simmonds (34) and 2nd engineer Robert Nibblett (25); from the *Wastdale H* mate Jack Dudfield (46), engineer Alex Bullock (40) and deckhand Malcolm Hart (17) were missing. It is known that Percy Simmonds was unable to swim and had entered the water with Jack Cooper, his body being recovered from the river on the Lydney side the following day. The other four crewmen missing were last seen on the bow of their vessels before being taken by the tide into the railway bridge, killed by the collision and explosion.

That same morning at 7.30. the Fire Service and Police, accompanied by the Sharpness Harbourmaster, walked out to the stranded barges. About half a mile from shore the *Arkendale H* lay on an even keel whilst the *Wastdale H* lay on her starboard side. Due to the incoming tide and the difficulty of walking on the mud, sandbanks and quicksand, it was decided to abandon any search until the following day.

During the following morning it proved to be difficult to search the vessels owing to the amount of oil and water in the barges. Arrangements were made that day for the transportation of light pumps out to the wrecks to enable the oil and water to be pumped out.

At 7.00 a.m. on Friday 28 October all the pumps had been assembled on the shore at Purton ready to be taken out to the wrecked vessels. Due to the strong tides of the previous couple of days the *Wastdale H* had regained an even keel and was surrounded by water to a depth of 2m. The job of getting the pumps out to the barges proved to be far more difficult than anticipated; they had been placed on makeshift wooden sledges and pulled across the mud, but halfway across they began to sink into the sand, almost disappearing into the quicksand. On arrival at the vessels it was only possible to get on board by clambering up the railway lines that still lay across the barges. A search was hampered still by the presence of oil, water and now fumes in both tanker barges and the operation was once again abandoned until the following day.

The Chief Fire Officer sought the co-operation of the RAF to airlift a special pump from Purton onto the deck of the *Wastdale H*, but that day dawned with news that the helicopter had developed engine trouble and was not available. Orders were given to manhandle the pump across the sands to the barge, where it was used to pump out all the oil and water whereupon a full search with firemen in breathing apparatus revealed nothing. A similar operation on the *Arkendale H* proved impossible due to her being holed below the waterline. So men with probes prodded into the engine room as best they could. At 11.00 a.m. that day all men and equipment were removed from the vessels due to the incoming tide.

The two tanker barges the day following the Severn Bridge Disaster.

On Sunday 30 October between 7.00 a.m. and 11.30 a.m. the wrecks were blown up with a series of small explosions to prevent their movement in the river, where, at low water, they can still be seen today.

The missing men were eventually all recovered from locations along the Severn Estuary.

An official inquiry into the accident between the two vessels and the Severn Railway Bridge was conducted at Bristol in May 1961 before Waldo Porges QC. During the three-day hearing Maurice Edwards, Senior Nautical Surveyor from the Ministry of Transport, showed concern for the safety of the River Severn and was perturbed at these casualties following so soon after the loss of the *BP Explorer* in the Severn Estuary with five men.

Waldo Porges QC in his summing up said, 'The disaster occurred without any fault in navigation for which either master can be blamed.' The Court recommended that all concerned in the administration of the harbour and approaches should consider it a matter of joint responsibility to examine the whole situation in detail with a view to improving existing conditions.

The Severn Railway Bridge: History & Demolition

The Building of the Bridge

On Thursday 18 July 1872 the Severn Bridge Railway Co. was formed to provide a link for the Great Western and the Severn & Wye Railway at Lydney to the Midland Railway at Sharpness. This would be of benefit to the Midland Railway as construction of the new dock at Sharpness had begun the previous year and the railway company saw the potential of bringing coal in from the Forest of Dean.

Following three years of planning, construction finally began in 1875 to the design of Mr T.E. Harrison. The contract for building the bridge was awarded to Hamiltons Windsor Iron Works Co. Ltd of London. A small gathering of local people had met on the foreshore at Purton (Lydney side) to witness the laying of the foundation stone at precisely 2.00 p.m. on Thursday 3 July 1875, by Mr W.C. Lucy, chairman of the Severn Bridge Railway Co., who made the speech expected at these occasions before laying the 2 ton block on solid rock.

Then followed four years of construction, sometimes not always going to plan, with certain work falling behind schedule, but, having overcome the might of the powerful tides of the Severn, the bridge was finally built. From the Lydney shore twelve masonry arches crossed the mudflats, then the three-quarter mile wide river was bridged by twenty-one spans, with a swing bridge crossing the Gloucester & Sharpness Ship Canal. Sadly, as was the case then with constructing something as large as this, fatalities occurred.

The first happened on Tuesday 8 January 1878 when workman John Tomkins of Ruardean was killed, not on the bridge, but at the nearby tunnel workings at Purton (Lydney side), when a section of timber weighing one ton fell on him when the securing rope slipped. A foreman employed by the tunnel construction company was severely reprimanded by the coroner for his lack of attention to safety and supervision.

A year later, on Wednesday 1 March, William Aston, aged sixty-four of Lydney, was killed in a fall on the viaduct at Purton (Lydney side). The inquest at Lydney Police Station was told that William Aston and a young chap called Drew were operating a travelling crane carrying

The magnificent Severn Railway Bridge soon after it was built. Taken from the Lydney side looking towards Sharpness.

stone blocks along the viaduct. The crane travelled on rails and as it was in the centre of the viaduct a strong wind blew up for about ten minutes. The crane was caught by the wind making it travel too fast along the rails until it crashed into some timber staging, falling 70ft to the deck below. Aston was thrown 25ft onto the staging and suffered serious injuries, whilst his mate, Drew, escaped injury. William Aston was removed to the new Severn Bridge Station where he died at 1.40 p.m.

The third and final fatality occurred as the end of construction of the bridge was in sight. It happened on Saturday 3 June 1879, as Thomas Roberts of Viney Hill fell from the bridge into the river whilst engaged in the erection of the last 312ft span. As he fell, he struck the staging causing him severe injuries, but was only in the river for five minutes as an alert boatman had spotted him falling and was able to rescue him. He died shortly after being taken to the Engineer's Rooms at Purton Manor.

The first train to test the bridge left Lydney Station at lunchtime on Wednesday 3 September 1879 with directors and managers of the companies involved travelling in a luxurious carriage to Sharpness. On the return trip at 2.30 p.m. the train stopped at the bridge to allow the passengers to alight and inspect the magnificent bridge.

The first collision with the bridge by a boat could be logged as happening on Saturday 6 September 1879. Thomas Shaw from Gatcombe, proprietor of a fishing business, together with his brother William and friend Thomas Margrate, had been at Avonmouth to purchase an anchor for one of their boats. Returning back to Gatcombe on a strong tide they made an effort to run through No.19 span of the Severn Railway Bridge, but as they rowed through they were caught in a large eddy and turned broadside across the tide. The large boat was taken out of control into the timber staging around the column, which subsequently cut it in two. All three men clung onto the staging, but that which Thomas Shaw was hanging onto collapsed, throwing him into the fast flowing tide, which then swept him away.

With some difficulty William Shaw and Thomas Margrate climbed the staging up onto the deck of the bridge and walked along the track to Sharpness, to the contractors office near to the old docks. Here they borrowed a boat to row back to the other side of the river and on up to Gatcombe. The following day divers searched the staging below water level to search for the missing body, but nothing was found. It was not until 9 September that the body of Thomas Shaw was recovered from the river by David Long of Framilode.

The great day finally arrived of the official opening of the Severn Railway Bridge on Friday 17 October 1879. Crowds of people gathered at both Sharpness and Lydney, with special trains bringing folk from Gloucester and elsewhere. A field at Sharpness had been turned into a fairground and on the other side of the river, the Lydney brass band turned out to add their bit to the occasion. The steam locomotive, *Maid Marian*, waiting at Lydney, was covered in bunting, as were the sides of the bridge. Even ships in the dock were dressed overall, with the grey clouds of the morning vanishing, giving way to clear skies and sun. Between 200 and 300 official guests gathered to see the chairman of the company, Mr W.C. Lucy, together with the Earl of Bathurst, the Earl of Ducie, Mr F. Allport, Mr G.W. Keeling and Mr W.P. Price climb aboard *Maid Marian* at noon, ready for the trip across the bridge. With whistle blowing, the steam train slowly pulled away out onto the bridge to fire its own royal salute, as fog signals had been placed on the line, one each side of the twenty-one spans.

After a brief halt at Sharpness, the train once again crossed the bridge. At the first 312ft span, however, the train stopped to allow Lucy to alight and tighten the last bolt on the bridge. When he completed this minor task he declared the bridge open for rail traffic.

Coincidentally, the date of the opening of the bridge, Friday 17 October 1879, was exactly one hundred years after the completion of that other great bridge on the Severn, Iron Bridge, the first bridge to be built of iron in England.

Demolition of the Bridge

A year after the disaster of 1960 there was mixed feelings about whether the bridge should be rebuilt or demolished. To rebuild the bridge would have cost £312,000 against an estimated cost of £250,000 to demolish it. Local feelings leaned towards rebuilding the bridge, as it had provided a vital link between the communities of Sharpness and Lydney. The Education Committee of Gloucestershire County Council were worried about the affect on transporting the children to each side of the river; until the accident schoolchildren from Sharpness had used the daily train to take them to and from Lydney Grammar School. Maj. E. Mealing, chairman of the Highways Committee, said that considering the small difference of £60,000 between restoration and demolition he thought the British Transport Commission should rebuild the bridge.

Whatever the outcome of the BTC's decision on rebuilding or demolishing the bridge, it had to be made safe so, in early December 1961, an underwater examination of the piers was carried out. Extensive damage to pier sixteen was found, it was leaning towards the Sharpness bank and in danger of collapsing into the river. A contract was awarded to Peter Lind & Co. Ltd to erect a temporary trestle under the bridge close to the damaged pier, and many people considered this to be the first stage of the reconstruction of the bridge.

Days before the company began work on erecting the trestle, another drama took place out in the river. On Friday 17 February 1961 an upturned tanker barge drifted out of control and struck pier twenty as it came downriver on the ebbing tide. Then on the next tide this same hulk drifted back upriver with the incoming flow and floated through the bridge to finally rest on the mud at Awre. It was estimated that this incident had added another £12,740 worth of damage to the bridge.

Peter Lind & Co. had hired, at a cost of £375 per week, a twin-hulled floating crane from Liverpool, named *Tweedledum & Tweedledee*. This was to be the cause of yet another calamity on the Severn for, on Friday 14 April 1961, this too broke away from its anchorage near to the bridge and drifted upriver on the flood tide. Soon after the alarm was raised at Sharpness, men boarded a small vessel, the *Magpie*, and set off to Awre where the floating crane had drifted to. Unfortunately a rope became entangled in the propeller of the *Magpie*, so all her crew could do was to stand and watch as the *Tweedledum & Tweedledee* floated back down river towards the bridge.

Once again the bridge was hit, the floating crane hit the dolphins on pier twenty hard, with the jib of the crane striking the underside of the bridge. The crane created another £6,000 worth of damage to the bridge as well as serious damage to herself, requiring a spell at Avonmouth Docks for repair. Back at the bridge, new moorings for the *Tweedledum & Tweedledee* had been devised to prevent another serious disaster happening. Fortunately this part of the contract was coming to an end, although it would still be some time before any definite decision was made on the future of the bridge.

Following the Severn Bridge Disaster of 25 October 1960 companies wanted compensation for damage to the bridge, loss of material and other costs. The case between John Harker Ltd and the British Transport Commission began in the courts during 1961. Others came to the court to make their claim; the Fairfield Shipbuilding & Engineering Co. Ltd, South West Gas Board and the Postmaster General. Fairfield's claim was for £8,704 10s 8d, but when the proceedings came to an end all they were awarded was a little over £100, with British Rail getting an award of £5,000.

Each year discussions took place as to what the future of the bridge would be, with many options being discussed. In 1965 the army were invited to the bridge to discuss the prospect of them demolishing the bridge. Plans of the bridge were scrutinised in great detail by the army, but any thoughts of carrying out a military exercise in demolition were ultimately dropped.

That same year twenty-four companies were asked to submit a tender for the demolition of the bridge, among them Underwater Welders Ltd of Cardiff and a local Sharpness company, IPL Shipyards. A site meeting had been arranged for 3 and 4 March to allow these companies a chance to see for themselves what the demolition job entailed. After this visit twenty of the twenty-four companies withdrew their bids!

The company which finally won the contract was Nordman Construction Co. Ltd of Gloucester, although not one of the original twenty-four companies asked to tender. Nordman's tender, when accepted, was the lowest.

During 1967 Nordman Construction announced to the press that demolition would be starting soon and that a huge floating crane from Hamburg, the *Magnus II*, would be used on the project. The *Magnus II* arrived on Tuesday 22 August at 9.30 a.m., piloted up the Severn estuary by a local man, Doug Griffey of Sharpness. This huge floating crane was considered to be the best there was, with a lifting capacity of 400 tons to a height of 150ft, self-propelled with four propellers, one on each corner of the hull and ballast tanks to ensure she kept on an even keel. The cost to hire though, was expensive, over £1,000 per day, thus the demolition company made plans to get the most work out of her in as less time as possible.

However, their plans went terribly wrong; the *Magnus II* worked in the river from 23 August until she left on 11 September, at a total cost of £21,000 and left behind twenty-one piers, three spans and the swing bridge still standing in the river!

All was not well, Nordman Construction were getting behind with the planned time schedule of the demolition of the bridge and viaduct, giving cause for concern to the district civil engineer. He demanded an explanation from the demolition company as to why the viaduct would not be demolished by 31 December.

It was agreed that the viaduct would have to be blown up and Swinnerton & Miller Ltd of Willenhall were sub-contracted to do the job. On 10 March 1968, not quite three months after the original deadline for the demolition of the viaduct, explosives were been placed in the stonework. The whole operation had been treated as top secret and at 7.30 a.m., under the glare of floodlights, the silence was broken by the first blast. Finally the viaduct was gone, just a mass of rubble and stone lying in the mud.

Demolition work had been going on for eight months; with no sign of the slick operation planned by Nordman Construction Co. Ltd and still no end in sight of when the bridge would be finally demolished. To add to their worries a request for £30,000 as an interim payment was refused. Then it was learned that Ulrich Harms, owner of the floating crane, *Magnus II*, was taking them to court for non-payment of their bill.

Eventually the receivers were called in to decide that Nordman Construction Co. Ltd would go into liquidation and take no further part in the demolition of the bridge. This left British Railways the problem of finding another company willing to carry on with the demolition of the bridge.

Swinnerton & Miller agreed terms to carry on with the demolition and used the ex Beachley-to-Aust ferryboat, *Severn King*, to assist with the operation. A crane had been placed on the vessel's deck turntable and this proved useful in lifting steel from the river into waiting barges. On the night of Friday 4 July 1969 disaster was to strike again when the *Severn King* broke adrift on a large tide and became impaled on the stump of pier number two. At low water the damage was found to be excessive. With the tides dropping and a large hole in the hull it meant that there was no chance of floating her off the pier, so temporary repairs were made to the hull before awaiting a suitable tide in which to float her off. On the evening of 28 July the *Severn King* was refloated and towed to the shore by Sharpness Piers and subsequently scrapped.

The end was finally in sight, for on Sunday 25 January 1970 the last remaining part of the Severn Railway Bridge was removed. It had been an elegant bridge with a history unmatched by any other that crosses the Severn. It is sad that it is only remembered for tragedy and not for the joy it had given many people as they travelled over it on the train, with a wonderful view of the river far below.

Chapter Three

George Thompson

Born 1927 in the small Yorkshire town of Maltby, George Thompon left school at fourteen years of age and went down the pits. One of his passions as a young teenager was boxing, proving himself to be quite a good fighter as an amateur boxer. Away from boxing young George would enjoy the company of his mates, making their own amusements in the difficult pre-war days. It was during this period that he met and fell in love with Doreen, a young girl living in the village of Conisborough.

George hated working in the pits, but with the outbreak of war he had no choice but to stick at it, for he had to sign on as a Bevan Boy, which classed as military service. His hatred of working in the pits drove him to run away to London on three occasions, each time getting caught by the authorities and returned to Yorkshire.

During 1949 George and Doreen got married in her local church at Conisborough and set off for their honeymoon in Gloucester, staying quite close to the docks. Nine months later saw them both in Gloucester again, this time for good. It had been decided on a toss of a coin between emigrating to Australia on the ten pound assisted scheme or coming to Gloucester (where Doreen had relatives) to work. Ironically George was offered two jobs, one at the local gas works and the other at Parker's Laundry in Ryecroft Street. The gas works paid more money, but when he saw that it entailed digging coal into bags, he opted for the cleaner laundry work!

Whilst on a short trip home to Yorkshire he found himself in a local pub at Knottingley, not far from the John Harker Shipyard. There he joined in a game of darts with a stranger, who as it turned out, was Fred Collins, manager of the Severn operations of the Harker tanker barge fleet. Fred Collins advised George to call in and see him on his return to Gloucester where there could be a vacancy as a crewman on one of the barges. George took him at his word and soon after his return to Gloucester presented himself in the managers office at the docks. Unfortunately he became too familiar with the manager, addressing him as Fred! Consequently Mr Collins showed him the door saying that there were no vacancies. Disappointed, George realised his stupidity and a few days later returned and apologised to Fred Collins, who accepted this and gave him a job as fourth hand on the *Westerndale H*.

Bill Merrett was skipper, a hard man who told George in no uncertain terms that he was there to clean the brass and do the cleaning. During the seven weeks that George was on the barge it was hard and at times unpleasant work. Whilst the other three crewmen would be able to go home when at Gloucester, he had orders to remain onboard and keep the barge warm and clean. One day, as the *Westerndale H* was tying up at Gloucester, skipper Bill Merrett was rather strict on George and told him that he was not to go home, but to remain onboard and clean out the accommodation. That trip, though, the engineer had decided to stay onboard, so he told George to discreetly slip home and that he would clean the vessel.

Skipper George Thompson on the deck of a tanker barge at Newport.

Sadly for George, the engineer knocked over a paraffin fire and burnt himself, thus incurring more wrath from the skipper!

Soon, though, he secured a mate's berth on the small tanker barge, *Severn Carrier*, with her skipper Harry Tonks, operating on the Avonmouth-to-Stourport run with just the crew of two men. Harry had a reputation for being a difficult person to work with, but fortunately George knew how to handle him, not like the mate sent to replace him during a period of leave. Just before George was due to report back to work the assistant manager went to his house to ask him to go to Avonmouth to join the barge there immediately. On his arrival he looked over the quay wall to see skipper Harry Tonks chasing the relief mate around the deck of the barge with an axe. A few words from George calmed the situation down and off they sailed up the Severn Estuary for the long trip to Stourport.

Whilst working for John Harker Ltd on the River Severn, George was more commonly known as Horace, a name he never really liked, so for the last twenty years he has preferred to be called George. Although as many a fourth hand will recall, he would only be called skipper by these young lads, to call him by his Christian name would ensure suffering the wrath of his tongue. Many Harker men were known by their nicknames, names like Longhair, Scouser and George. Well his was Oscar. Why? According to him, a shortened version of Horace.

From the *Severn Carrier* George went to another small tanker barge, this time to skipper the *Severn Rover*. His mate was to be Brian Everett, for both men their first time in their promoted positions. During this period he became the first man to take a barge over every weir from Stourport to Gloucester whilst the river was in flood. Not without an incident though, for as he rounded the bend to go towards the weir he suddenly saw a footbridge across the river in front of him. No time for fear, only to duck and hope the barge would go under. It did, but only just!

Another weir episode occurred when he came out of the Upper Parting at Gloucester to see the large *Shell Roadbuilder* drifting powerless down the cutting towards Maisemore Weir. Without hesitation George turned the little *Severn Rover* into the same cutting and swung his barge around, but the force of the current was dragging the barge down to and close to going over the weir. Coming down river, empty, was the small tanker barge, *Huntdale H*, and when her skipper, Aubrey Everett, saw their predicament, he dropped stern first down towards the two barges. He put a rope onto the *Severn Rover* and assisted in towing the *Shell Roadbuilder* away from the weir.

George remained skipper of the *Severn Rover* for a further three years, until the Suez crisis temporarily closed down petroleum depots at Stourport during the 1950s. With a juggling of crews by the company, George was offered the mate's job on the *Wyesdale H* and then mate on the *Widdale H*.

It was as mate on the *Widdale H* that disasters were to form a large piece of George Thompson's life whilst working on the River Severn and Bristol Channel. The 400 ton tanker

Skipper George Thompson at the wheel of the Wyesdale H *Sailing empty down the Bristol Channel to Swansea.*

John Harker tanker barge Widdale H *leaving the Queen's Dock, Swansea, loaded bound for Sharpness.*

barge *Widdale H* had been built in 1954 at Knottingley, Yorkshire, and carried a crew of four, skipper, mate, engineer and fourth hand, usually referred to as the boy. On 1 April 1959 the tanker barge had left Swansea with a cargo of premium spirit bound for Worcester. When going through the narrow channel at the Nash, thick fog descended and the *Widdale H* touched a sandbank and grounded on the bottom. The coastal tanker *Regent Jane* stood by whilst the skipper of the *Widdale H* tried to get his vessel off the sandbank, but as the tide was ebbing away this proved to be impossible. Apart from the fog, weather conditions were good; a light wind with a calm sea, no worries of damage to the barge, which only had to wait for the next tide to float off.

Between tides fate played a cruel trick, for the wind increased to gale force and as the tide turned and the *Widdale H* rose off the sand, the wind drove her closer to the rocks at the foot of the Nash cliffs. Another tanker barge came on the scene, the *Shell Roadbuilder*, her crew launched a life raft, but the vicious seas stopped them from reaching the stricken barge. According to the mate, George Thompson, the sea did the rest. The 20ft swell drove the tanker barge steadily towards the shore and for several hours it was pounded by the sea against the rocks at the foot of the 150ft cliff. As the cargo tanks ruptured the fumes entered the engine-room causing the main engine to race wildly out of control. Everything possible was done to shut down the engine but to no avail, and it still raced away at an alarming speed;

the crew thought it would blow up at any moment taking the rest of the barge with it. In front of the wheelhouse was a small well-deck where George Thompson came across Alec Bullock up to his thighs in pure premium spirit laughing and joking, drunk from the fumes, encouraging George to come and join him.

At low water all four crew members, skipper Stanley Hodgson, mate George Thompson, engineer Alec Bullock and deckhand Winston Howe, all from Gloucester, made a scramble for the shore. They were all nearly overcome by fumes from the ruptured cargo tanks making them giddy as though they were drunk. As the crew arrived at the foot of the cliffs the local Fire Brigade were there to help pull them to the top, where they were assessed for injuries and taken to Bridgend Hospital.

The *Widdale H* had been carrying a cargo of 341 tons of motor spirit from Swansea to Worcester, the value of the cargo was worth £27,000. All vessels were warned to keep clear of the area as the petrol fumes could be smelt sixteen miles away. A decision had to be taken soon whether to let the *Shell Roadbuilder* attempt to tow the stricken barge off the rocks. She had become embedded in shingle and pebbles under the cliff and it had been hoped to tow her off the beach at high water the day following the grounding. Gloucester Shipyard fitter Fred Green had devised a plan whereby holes in the stricken vessel would be plugged and then to float lines out to sea with life-rings attached. Standing by at sea would be the *Shell Roadbuilder* which would pick up the lines and attempt to pull the *Widdale H* off the beach. The salvaged vessel would then proceed to Sully, near Cardiff, where she would be beached near the hospital.

The *Widdale H* lay alongside a large rock and as Fred Green was working on the deck he glanced up and saw a large wave approaching, whereby he made a dash for the safety of the wheelhouse. Only just in time for the wave lifted the tanker barge up and dropped her stern neatly onto the rock. Looking into the engine room Fred could see an 8ft gash with water pouring in. Thus all attempts to plug the holes had been unsuccessful.

On 8 April it was decided to abandon any hope of refloating her. She had been heavily damaged by the high waves and gales of the last few days and was now firmly entrenched in a bed of pebbles at the foot of the cliff. The engine of the *Widdale H* was salvaged and used again in another tanker barge, her hull was cut up by a salvage company from Swansea and taken away for scrap.

George Thompson was offered mate's job on the *Arkendale H*, built in 1937 at Lowestoft as a dumb barge before being rebuilt in 1948 as a motor barge. This tanker barge carried heavy black oil which necessitated her having to have a boiler with steam coils running through the cargo to keep the oil in a liquid state. After serving aboard with two different skippers, George became skipper of the *Arkendale H* himself and sadly she was to be involved in his next disaster, together with the Severn Railway Bridge and the *Wastdale H*.

After the Severn Bridge Disaster, when he returned to work George became skipper of the rebuilt *Wyesdale H*. The *Wyesdale H* had originally been built to trade only from Avonmouth to Worcester, built as a sister barge to the ill-fated *Wastdale H*, with a low bow making it too dangerous to trade down the Bristol Channel. During late 1960-early 1961 the *Wyesdale H* was rebuilt at Gloucester Shipyard with a raised bow to trade in the Bristol Channel as far down as Swansea and on the River Severn up to Worcester. It was when he was skipper of the *Wyesdale H* that George Thompson became involved in another tragedy on the night of

Sunday 19 November 1961, when proceeding down the Severn Estuary from Sharpness together with the *Wharfedale H*, both barges struck a rescue launch at the site of the new Severn Suspension Bridge.

From the *Wyesdale H* George with his crew moved to the *Rosedale H* and finally to the brand new tanker barge *Winsdale H*. Built in 1962 at Knottingley the crew joined her at Sharpness early in the cold winter of 1963. As was the case with the majority of the large John Harker barges, the accommodation was excellent, with each crew member having his own cabin. The *Winsdale H* was no exception, she was a warm and cosy vessel with a happy crew, a crew which had remained with George Thompson for the previous three years. But there remained one more disaster to test the strength of Capt. George Thompson.

During February 1970 the *Winsdale H* had been into Port Talbot to deliver a cargo of petroleum and although the weather was stormy, George decided to lock-out for the short run down to Swansea for collection of another cargo. Unfortunately as they left the lock at Port Talbot a wave lifted the tanker barge and the steering chain fell off the quadrant. This caused the *Winsdale H* to turn hard to starboard. Out of control, she became stranded on the sands of the nearby Aberavon Beach. The tides were beginning to neap (a tide just after the first or third quarters of the moon when there is least difference between high and low water) so, although she was being pounded by the waves, there was not enough water to pull her out to the safety of the sea. It was the low tides that saved her, for she was only feet away from being driven onto the concrete sea wall at Aberavon! A couple of the crew were taken off for their own safety and later, as the tides increased, a tug from Alexandra Towing Co. pulled her off the sands. She remained in the fleet until the company ceased trading in the Severn area in 1971.

Following many years of trading on the United Kingdom's waterways, John Harker was slowly losing contracts in the early 1970s to other operators. Thus it was that George Thompson decided to take the redundancy package offered by the company in 1971. Six months later Harker's had finished trading on the Severn, together with other barge operators in this area, the new motorway and oil pipeline killing off all trade on Britain's rivers.

Not letting this sad period get him down, George applied to the old Bristol company of Sand Supplies (Western) Ltd for a job on their sand dredgers. First he was on the little *Sand Pearl* which had been converted from a coal barge and then he was made skipper of the ex-Dutch coaster *Sand Jade*. A nasty accident occurred one day whilst dredging for sand near to the Holms, located in the Bristol Channel midway between Cardiff and Weston-Super-Mare, when, as the suction pipe was being raised off the sea bed, a rope snapped. It lashed out and sliced off George's nose leaving it hanging by a thread from his face. Calmly he went to his cabin, looked in the mirror and could see that it was serious! A call was made on the radio asking the Barry Pilot Boat to assist to transport him to the nearest hospital. Still in high spirits whilst on the Pilot Boat, George could see the apprentice pilot looking inquisitively at his face. He dropped the bandage to expose his badly disfigured face whereupon the boy fainted. After a short time spent in a Cardiff Hospital the nose had been sewn back on and now only a small scar remains.

From the *Sand Jade* he progressed as skipper of the larger *Sand Sapphire* and finally skipper of the fairly new *Sand Diamond*. Sadly this work ceased in 1990 when the company finally wound up its operations in the Bristol Channel. Their Bristol site at Hotwells was sold for a new housing complex.

The loaded Widdale H *on the rocks at the foot of the cliff at The Nash.*

George Thompson was asked to deliver two redundant sand dredgers to Bahrain. First he took the *Harry Brown* from Barry to Ireland for a small refit, before sailing to the Middle East, but this trip unfortunately had a sad episode. In the Mediterranean, the mate Scouser (John Samson) was found to be missing. Following an extensive search of the ship he was presumed to have fallen overboard.

The second vessel he delivered was the *Sand Sapphire*, also from Barry, this time with no mishaps!

Not one to be idle and realising he is too old for rushing about on ships and barges, he has taken on an active role in the community where he and Doreen live, as a Gloucester City Councillor. It allows him to spend time with his family (two sons, a daughter and grandchildren plus great-grandchildren). Perhaps all his disasters are behind him?

Chapter Four
Ivor Price Langford,
Ship Repairer, Sharpness Docks

A well respected local shipyard, Ivor Price Langford did much to avert disasters on the Severn, especially with their involvement in the story of the grounding of the steam freighter *Stancliffe* in 1947.

3 April 1947 – Stancliffe, *Aground off Sharpness*

The winter of 1947 produced record floods on the River Severn. Following a long spell of snow and ice, a rapid thaw set in sending torrents of water down the river, with the effect noticed at Sharpness, where out in the estuary, sandbanks were not showing at the tidal low water mark.

A British ship, the 1,580 ton *Stancliffe*, slowly made her way up the Severn Estuary to Sharpness on the evening tide of 3 April 1947. The *Stancliffe*, owned by J. Bilmier & Co. of London, was carrying a cargo of 700 standards of timber from Emden in Germany, amounting to a weight of about 3,000 metric tons. As she swung in the river to stem the tide before entering the port, the ship hit a tump of sand and grounded a little way north of Sharpness Piers.

Soon, with the tidal force of this region, she heeled over to a forty-five degree angle causing her deck lashings to break and loose many tons of timber into the river.

On the morning tide of the following day, five tugs were sent up to Sharpness to try to pull the *Stancliffe* off the mudbank, but were unsuccessful. Her crew of thirty-five were taken off the freighter by tug, because of the risk of the ship capsizing, and stood by ashore. At such short notice it was difficult to find accommodation for them all and half the crew were accommodated at Sharpness Seamen's Mission, the remainder staying at the Towers Hotel, Newport, Gloucestershire.

As the Thursday evening tide flooded in, another attempt was made to pull her off, this time using only four tugs. The ship floated, but developed such a heavy list to starboard that it became impossible to dock her at Sharpness. Whilst afloat the *Stancliffe* swung with the tide, but her two anchors, each with forty-five fathoms paid out, prevented her from drifting. Now she lay a further 200 yards north of the pier and it was decided to abandon operations for the night.

The following day was Good Friday and, as the morning tide came in, the stricken vessel was down by the head with the rising waters swinging the stern around. But, as the tide ebbed, the ship righted herself and swung back to her original position, remaining on an even keel on the mud.

The Stancliffe *aground off Sharpness and split in two, with a tug alongside.*

A call had gone out to Southampton asking for the assistance of salvage experts, who arrived later that Friday. They discovered that the ship had undergone terrific straining to the hull, which had caused several small leaks into her foreholds. To avoid the *Stancliffe* from swinging again on subsequent tides, which would cause further stress to the hull, it was decided to flood all cargo holds to hold the ship firmly on the bed of the river.

The Liverpool Salvage Association was called in to make an attempt to salvage the vessel, their first task being to stop her floating again on the tides. It was they who cut holes in the side of the hull to flood the cargo holds, but as they were too small, the ship refloated and drifted into a far worse position. Where she lay now was preventing large ships from entering Sharpness, a cause for concern for the Gloucester Harbour Board, the controlling authority for managing navigation in the Severn Estuary.

Their plan had been to remove the cargo of timber over the following few days, seal the holes in the hull, pump out the river water and hopefully dock her at Sharpness. Nature chose differently though, for as the tides raced in twice per day they began to take their toll on the ship. Soon she had broken her back, with a split from gunwale to bilge keel on both port and starboard side. Now the *Stancliffe* was officially declared a 'total loss' and abandoned by the insurance underwriters after they had been advised that salvage of the ship was impracticable. Only her steam engine was considered not to have suffered any damage and worthy of recovery.

The ship was not completely broken in two, for the forward and stern sections were still connected by her deck plates. But the risk was too high and with little chance of making any profit, the Liverpool Salvage Association gave up their attempt to salvage the *Stancliffe*.

However, one man never gave up hope of salvaging the ship, local Sharpness engineer, Ivor 'Tyke' Langford, owner of Ivor Price Langford, Ship Repairer, Sharpness.

Two months later the Gloucester Harbour Board was worried about the problems the ship was causing to other vessels entering and leaving the dock at Sharpness. They arranged for Langford's ship repairing company to move the wreck away from the entrance to the dock. Under Ivor's supervision the ship was beached on mud flats away from the piers. The ship was held together with steel hawsers through each side of the split, forward of the bridge. In fact the *Stancliffe* was literally 'stitched' together with the steel hawsers, as Ivor was of the opinion that if she was floated 'rigid' then she may possibly break apart.

The months passed into the following year without any more salvage work being carried out on the wreck. Then during January 1948 the Newbigin Steam Shipping Co. Ltd of Newcastle-upon-Tyne purchased the wreck as she lay out in the mud of the Severn. They had a belief that the *Stancliffe* could be salvaged and with Langford's confidence awarded him the job of getting the wreck off the mud. At noon on 15 January the wreck was insured again on the Marine Market, believed at the time to be the first time this had happened. The underwriters would only agree to cover the risk on condition that Capt. H.B. Mylchreest of London, advisor to Lloyd's of London, supervised operations. The policy stated that the insurance was to continue until Harold Mylchreest & Co. had given the vessel's two sections a seaworthiness certificate for towage to a port of delivery.

Ivor Langford gathered together a workforce of thirty men and on 17 January 1948 began work on the wreck. Welders, riveters, platers, and carpenters all worked on the main task, to make the hull watertight. The work went on relentlessly, day and night, through to the end

The stern section of the Stancliffe.

A close view of the split of the Stancliffe.

of February. Steel bulkheads were fitted either side of the split, holes in the hull patched over and valves installed to control the intake and output of water. After all this hard work had been completed and it was proved that the ship would float, the only remaining task for Ivor and his men was to cut the deck plating and wire hawsers to separate the ship into two parts.

Crowds gathered on the foreshore of the morning of Saturday 28 February 1948 to see the stern part of the *Stancliffe* begin her journey away from Sharpness, the port she never did manage to berth at! Three large tugs from Avonmouth came to tow the vessel away, the *Fairplay 3* acting as bow tug, which slowly moved into the muddy, swirling deep water off Sharpness. At high water the *Stancliffe* came off the mud and swung around to lay astern of the *Fairplay 3*, tow rope straining against the strength of the tide. Towing her rudder first, the other two tugs took up their station at the stern as the hull was slowly moved down the Severn Estuary. Steam had been raised on the *Stancliffe* and as she vanished into the morning mist blew a fond farewell to Sharpness on her whistle. Those watching from the shore were unaware how close it had been for the pilots to call off the trip due to the mist.

The stern section of the *Stancliffe* arrived at Cardiff at about 9.30 that evening after experiencing patchy fog in the Bristol Channel. If they had waited until the Sunday to commence the trip it would have surely been called off, as the fog was much worse!

During the middle of March the same exercise was carried out, this time towing the bow section of the *Stancliffe* to Cardiff Docks. A letter to Ivor Langford, dated Tuesday 2 March 1948, from the Newbiggin Steam Shipping Co. Ltd, gave praise for his efforts in salvaging the stern section of the *Stancliffe* and trusted that he would have the bow section ready for towing by 12 or 13 March.

Ivor was also given praise by the villagers at Sharpness, one dockyard worker stating that, but for his foresight and hard work, the *Stancliffe* may have become a total wreck.

In fact the *Stancliffe* was rebuilt at Cardiff and then promptly renamed *Gripfast*, perhaps in recognition of the Severn mud holding her fast for ten months. The Newbiggin Steam Shipping Co. Ltd traded with the ship for a further twelve years until selling her to a Panamanian-flagged shipping company. Eventually the sea was to claim her though, for after a further nineteen years of trading she sank in 1967.

Stancliffe

Built 1941 as the *Empire Brook*.
Owned by J. Bilmier & Co. of London.
Built by W. Gray & Co. Ltd, Hartlepool.
2,866 grt, 321ft long, 44ft wide.
Fitted with a three-cylinder steam engine.
1948 Sold as wreck to Newbiggin Steam Shipping Co. Ltd of Newcastle-upon-Tyne.
1948 Renamed *Gripfast*.
1960 Renamed *Capetan Costas P* (Panamanian flag).
1966 Renamed *Karine M* (Panamanian flag).
1967 Renamed *Pitsa* (Panamanian flag).
12 December 1967 The ship foundered after developing uncontrollable leaks. She was being towed by a motor salvage tug from Djibouti to Colombo when she sank.

Ivor Price Langford (1901-1980)

Ivor was born into an established Sharpness family. During his schooldays he could be seen bunking off school, swimming in the log pond on the canal at Purton or out in the Severn fishing for salmon with his lave net. His mother would then teach him how to sell the fish and save the money for a rainy day.

At the age of fourteen he went down to Barry and joined the little pilot cutter *Alaska*. With the apprentice already on board they waited for the crew to join them from the local pub. As soon as they were aboard ropes were cast off and out into the Bristol Channel they went. Unfortunately a severe gale was blowing and young Ivor was shoved into the cabin and told to keep out of the way. The gale was so severe that they had to turn around and run back to Barry.

Ivor's dad was a channel pilot and on the occasions when he would take a vessel up to Lydney Dock, Ivor would have to row a punt across the estuary to bring his dad back to Sharpness.

Ivor, with his mop of red hair, was physically strong with a fiery temperament to match. His nickname 'Tyke' was given to him because of his activities around the dock. Once, he built a small rowing boat and rounded up a few of the local children and took them out on the river in it, much to the dismay of the children's mothers who looked on in horror.

Ivor left the pilot cutter after a number of years of sailing the Bristol Channel to serve his time at Sharpness drydock, then operated by Cardiff Channel Drydock Co. When the depression came he went off to Canada at the age of twenty-one, gradually working his way across this vast country. One of the many jobs he found was as a dance hall bouncer, a time

Ivor Price Langford as a young man.

he subsequently related to his family of when it really was 'ten cents a dance' as the well-known song goes. He eventually found work on a farm at Saskatchewan where he stayed one year before joining an 'outfit' travelling around Canada harvesting wheat. Arriving at Nova Scotia one day he went to work in the local shipyard. After a while he decided it was time to return home to England so he joined a cattle ship, the *Canadian Leader*, as one of the firemen. Halfway through the voyage back to England, one of the engineers fell ill and because Ivor was indentured he was asked to take his place. Their first port was Dundee before sailing on to Cardiff where the chief engineer would not release Ivor so he promptly jumped ship!

He then married and lived back in Severn Road at Sharpness with his wife, Lilian. Together they raised their four children, Robert, Richard, Diana and Christina. It was not long before Ivor had built a shed on some wasteland near his home to set up a small business of repairing ships. Cardiff Channel Drydock Co. had by this time left the local shipyard but had left their buildings intact, complete with some machinery. Ivor took his opportunity and could often be seen clambering over the fence to use this redundant equipment. British Transport, who operated Sharpness Docks, asked Ivor if he would like to lease the drydock to repair ships. Part of this agreement was for Ivor to clean out the tons of mud and debris from the drydock and then pay a rent to use the facilities each time a ship came in for repair.

In 1941 he bought an old steam sand dredger, the *Kyles*, lying forlorn at Ilfracombe. He towed her to Sharpness and rebuilt her into a little coaster and secured a contract for carrying carbide from Port Talbot to Gloucester with a return cargo of grain from the Monk Meadow silo. Built in 1872 by Fullertons of Paisley, Scotland, her claim to fame was as being the oldest trading vessel still registered in Lloyds Shipping Register towards the end of her time at Sharpness during the late 1970s. During the 1960s, Langford's had a contract for taking gas water in the *Kyles* from Gloucester Gas Works for disposal at sea in the Bristol Channel off

Ivor Price Langford out hunting.

Avonmouth. With her crew of two, skippered by one of Ivor's two sons, she would leave Sharpness on one tide and return on the next.

Following the closure of Gloucester Gas Works, Ivor Langford began to carry waste chemical products for disposal at sea, now simply loading from a lorry at Sharpness Docks. To assist with this trade the company purchased another small coasting vessel, the *Fulham*, built as a water carrier for use during the Second World War and then named *Empire Fulham*. Being quite a modern vessel compared to the *Kyles* and, as it was seen that companies were now recycling the waste as opposed to dumping it at sea, only the *Fulham* was used on a regular basis. Then one day a ship swinging in the docks at Sharpness came too close to the *Kyles* and damaged her wheelhouse. It was time to sell her; it was a sad day at Sharpness as this little, old vessel sailed for the last time out of Sharpness, bound for Scotland (the *Kyles* is currently on display and open to the public at the Scottish Maritime Museum).

The last vessel the company bought was another little coastal tanker, the *New Start*, purchased with main engine seized. She was towed from Newport, where she had been lying idle for some considerable time. She was bought in 1979, a year before Ivor P. Langford peacefully passed away. Although his sons worked hard to restore the engine of the *New Start*, it became uneconomical to carry on so the ship was sold before carrying any cargo for the company.

Sadly on Friday 4 January 1980 Ivor died suddenly at Gloucestershire Royal Hospital and on this day as a mark of respect to this well-liked gentleman, a flag was flown at half-mast at the entrance to Sharpness Docks.

Ivor Price Langford in his mature years.

Ivor Price Langford with his Jaguar E-type sports car.

23 March 1951 – *The Loss of the* Ramses II.

A large 4,845 ton Egyptian-registered freighter, *Ramses II*, had come up the Severn Estuary, accompanied by two tugs from Avonmouth, a little late on one of the fortnightly strong spring tides bound for the port of Sharpness. As they approached Sharpness at 8.30 p.m. one of the large tugs secured her heavy tow rope to the bow of the ship, the other tug attaching her tow rope to the stern of the vessel. Ivor Langford was standing on the foreshore at Sharpness with his family that evening and commented to his daughter Diana, 'Much further over and she'll be aground.'

They were about to begin the customary swinging of the ship to stem the tide before entering Sharpness when the *Ramses II* touched Lydney Sand. The tugs let go their tow ropes and the steamship ended up in Wellhouse Bay, now at the mercy of the strong evening tide. With Severn pilot, Mr J. Morgan of Sharpness in charge, he gave orders for the wheel to be put hard over and with full speed tried to drive the ship around to avoid the sandbanks. Unable to get the ship's bow around into the tide quick enough without the aid of the bow tug, the ship grounded on Saniger Sands, midway between Sharpness and Lydney.

The *Ramses II* was carrying a cargo of 7,000 tons of maize from Russia for Severn Ports Warehousing Co. Ltd, Sharpness, not an ideal cargo to be carrying when a ship grounds. Both the pilot and the German captain struggled to free the ship, but with a falling tide had to abandon all hope of getting her afloat that night. The problem with a ship grounding out in the Severn, is that as the next tide races in there is a chance that the vessel will be held in the mud and not float as the water rises. With this thought in mind the captain of the *Ramses II* arranged to have his crew taken ashore.

During the following day observers on the shore could see that the ship had developed a large split in the hull amidships. Grain, being one of the most lucrative cargoes a ship will carry, brought the owners of the cargo to Sharpness to arrange for it to be taken off the grounded vessel, from where she lay in the estuary.

By Tuesday the *Ramses II* was firmly aground on Saniger Sands and it was decided that no further attempts would be made to salvage her. The owners of the grain had been successful in getting 6,000 tons of it off the ship before gales and wind plus the high tides had taken their

The Ramses II *soon after the ship grounded in the Severn off Sharpness.*

A view on board the Ramses II.

Workman on the deck of the stranded Ramses II.

Ramses II
Built 1924 as *Wansford*.
4,943 grt.
Fitted with a three-cylinder
steam engine.
1950 Sold to Mr A. Klat of
Alexandria, Egypt.

Above: *Water slopping over the decks
of the stranded* Ramses II.

Right: *A view of the* Ramses II *from
another vessel lying alongside.*

Grabbing out the cargo of grain from the Ramses II.

toll. Now the ship, deeper in the mud, had water in the engine room and crew's quarters. It was also noticed that some water had got into the holds and had begun to spoil the grain.

IPL Shipyards Ltd of Sharpness, with Ivor Langford in charge, took the little *Kyles* out in the river to begin cutting away and removing steel from the ship above her decks. Now the smell of rotting, damp grain could be smelt as it wafted over the port of Sharpness and the docks of Lydney to the west of the wreck.

For years the wreck of the *Ramses II* could be seen at low water in the mud of Saniger Sands. Now it is somewhat of a rare occurrence to view her from Sharpness Pier looking in the direction of Lydney Docks. After a storm or at low water following a large spring tide, the keen eye can just pick her out, fifty years after she first grounded in the Severn.

The wreck of the Ramses II *showing above the sands off Lydney, fifty years after she grounded.*

Chapter Five
Navigation

Although the River Severn is Britain's longest river, it has never been the easiest to navigate. Above Gloucester the river is naturally very shallow, causing many problems for traders over the centuries. Below Gloucester there is the added difficulty of the fierce tides racing up the estuary, filling the river in a matter of hours, then draining out again, leaving vast areas of sand banks exposed.

Before the building of motorways in England during the mid-twentieth century, Britain's rivers were the highways of the country, used for conveying goods in barges. From Roman times the Severn would have seen vessels trading along much of its length, carrying mostly raw materials. It is hard to imagine now, but small barges would trade inland, up the Severn as far as Pool Quay, a few miles below Welshpool. Traders here would have to wait for 'fresh water' (rain water coming down from the Welsh hills which raises the depth of the river above normal level) to return, and it was not unknown for a barge to be stranded on the bed of the river for over two months!

With no engine to move the barge along the river it would have been difficult taking a vessel from Gloucester all the way to Shropshire. At Gloucester the men would rely on the spring tides to carry them up as far as Worcester as well as using their sails, but above this city it was another story! Gangs of men, known as bow hauliers, would pull the barges upriver against a strong current. They were strong rough men, recruited, in the main, from Bewdley. It required twenty men in a gang to haul a laden vessel. In 1773 a towpath was built along the river to allow horses to tow the vessels, but this led to rioting by the bow hauliers, with the men of the Scots Greys being brought in to restore order.

The most important period for navigation on the Severn in and around Shrewsbury was during the mid-seventeenth and eighteenth centuries, especially with the growth of Ironbridge with its great smelting works. The trade then was long distance with vessels trading to Bristol, but due to the state of the river, many only managed one trip per year. Slowly things worsened as channels in the river were allowed to silt up and although a few remaining fish weirs assisted barges across the shallows, trade to this area finished by 1870.

River trade above Stourport started to come to an end during the late nineteenth century. The last of the trows would be carrying bricks and tiles from the Broseley district above Bridgnorth, but would not travel when the river was low, only when there was a flush of 2-3ft.

As they came down river loaded, through Bridgnorth Bridge, they did not stop on the quay, but kept going down with the current. Coming upriver empty they were towed by a horse and usually stopped at Bridgnorth for the night.

All this finished dramatically in 1895 when the last barge came down the river. As the barge was approaching Bridgnorth Bridge the attention of the steersman was distracted by a fall of rock into some cottages. The stern of the vessel hit the side of the bridge, which caused the barge to swing around towards the quay. A man jumped off the barge with a rope and others on the bank ran for help. Too late, the rope tightened and the barge sank about a hundred yards below the bridge.

The Government realised that something had to be done to open up the Severn as a commercial waterway, especially as the steam engine had been invented by now and steam tugs were appearing on the river. It was agreed to build a series of locks and weirs between Gloucester and Stourport, to raise the level of the river and in effect canalise the Severn between these two towns.

The problem with navigating the Severn below Gloucester is the tide. A vessel could run with the incoming tide to Gloucester, but could not go back down river all the way past Sharpness on the ebb. It would take two or three tides to travel back down river, un-economical for a trader who has to get his goods to market as quick as possible. Then there were the ever-changing sand banks, where barges would ground on the ebb, only to be capsized by the incoming tide. To make this a viable commercial waterway was one of the reasons why the sixteen-mile Gloucester & Berkeley Canal, later renamed the Gloucester & Sharpness Ship Canal, was opened in 1827 to bypass this treacherous part of the Severn.

Over a period of time many vessels sank along the course of the Severn, some resulting in the death of crewmen. Many of these mishaps would never have appeared in print, not as today when all such incidents are well documented. It was with the introduction of the petrol trade onto the River Severn in the 1920s that accidents of a serious nature began, no doubt not helped by the very nature of the volatile cargo carried in the tanker barges and the great number of these vessels continually travelling along the river from early morning until late at night.

A Typical Trip to Worcester

During the 1950s, as John Harker Ltd introduced their large tanker barges to the Severn area, the Bristol Channel down to Swansea was opened up. The lucrative Swansea-to-Worcester trip meant that a tanker barge could do two round trips a week, but only by working long hours and taking some risks. As the men were paid 'trip money' it wasn't unusual for them to work 110 hours each week, constantly trying to be first in the queue to load or discharge. The Gloucester & Sharpness Ship Canal could not be used at night, but the Severn above Gloucester could, as long as the management ordered the locks in advance.

Navigating the Severn Estuary is totally different to taking a barge on the river above Gloucester. In the estuary the bargeman had to contend with tides and his movements were restricted by the time of high water, twice in any twenty-four hour period, moving forward by half an hour each tide. Buoys, flashing away during the hours of darkness, mark the channel; nowadays the estuary is lit up like a Christmas tree, but this was not always the case. In recent years past, the lights were few and far between and on a dark, cloudy night it was a job to pick out one buoy to the next.

Leaving Avonmouth or approaching from Swansea, craft would take a northerly course heading for The Shoots, a narrow channel across which now is built the Second Severn Crossing bridge. On the port side is the small Denny Island, an area subject to shifting sands,

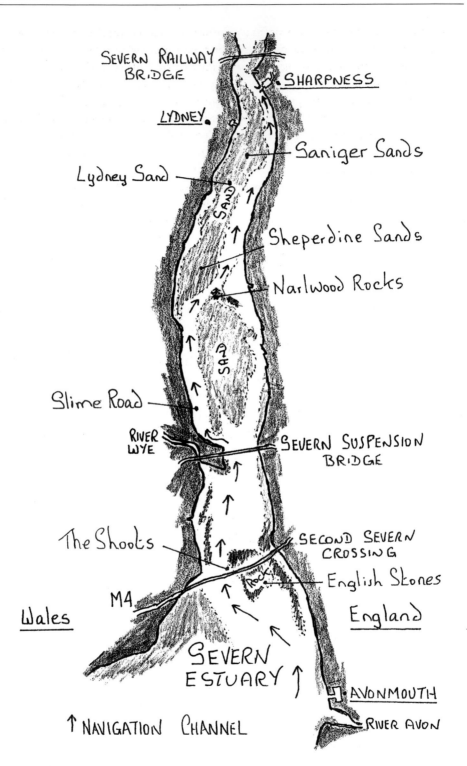

Map of the Severn Estuary from Avonmouth to Sharpness with the navigation channel indicated.

then the wide expanse of the Bedwin Sands, beautiful sands but woe betide the skipper who tries to take a short cut across them! The Second Severn Crossing is built across the English Stones, hard rock on the bed of the river, with the Severn Railway Tunnel running beneath. Always a turbulent waterway, with plenty of spray even on a calm day, and with a gale blowing men on small barges felt as though they were out in the North Atlantic!

The course would alter now, heading for the Severn Bridge, keeping close to the Beachley shore as they turned into Slime Road. There followed almost two miles of channel, hugging the shore along past Sedbury Cliffs, towards the Inward Rocks Light, two lights set apart from each other, known as 'leading lights'. When both are in line, the course alters to take the barge across the Severn. Half way across they would be looking for the Counts Light, marking the treacherous Narlwood Rocks, then passing on the starboard side the reservoir for Oldbury Power Station, marked by leading lights and a buoy marking the Ledges. Coming across the estuary, the man on the wheel of the barge would have difficulty in holding a straight course due to the force of the current sweeping over and at right angles to the channel. Ahead of them, at Sheperdine, would be another pair of leading lights, guiding them to the east bank of the Severn Estuary, the skipper then altering course to take them past the Hills Flats buoy.

In fog, men were wary about proceeding on to Sharpness, especially without radar (as the majority did not have even in the 1950s and 1960s). At Sheperdine, on the shore in front of the Windbound Public House, the bed of the river is hard and ideal for barges to lie to await the next tide, when hopefully the fog would have cleared. Hanging from one of the leading lights was a large ship's bell, rung in fog by local man Percy Palmer, to guide the barges to the safety of the shore. A crewman would be on the bow of the vessel shouting to the skipper when the sound was dead ahead. The bell was from a large sailing ship, the *Atlas*, built near Hull in 1812 and scrapped in 1832. Recovered from the ship, the bell found a new home in Gloucester Docks to be rung when summoning the dockers to work. In 1941 it was taken down to Sheperdine and hung on one of the 'Leading Lights' until the mid-1980s when it was again returned to Gloucester Docks to hang on the end of North Warehouse, the offices of Gloucester City Council. At low water the barge would be high and dry on the bottom, giving the chance for the crew to walk around the vessel, inspecting for any damage, especially to the propeller, which would always take a knock upriver above Gloucester.

Here at Sheperdine and over across at Slime Road were the only two safe places to lie out in the river at low water. Elsewhere in the estuary, as the barge touched bottom on the ebbing tide, it would be possible for the sandy bed to rise up to deck level on one side of the vessel and drop right away on the other. As the tide returned, flowing and rising fast as is normal for the Severn, the chances were that the barge would remain stuck in the sand, soon being completely covered by the rising tide. This is still the case today and, although pilotage is compulsory for commercial vessels, pilots are well aware of this danger and if the ship they are piloting gives any sign of engine failure, tugs are alerted to tow them to safety.

Passing Sheperdine the channel hugs the shore, passing more leading lights at Hayward Rock and Berkeley Power Station (now decommissioned) before reaching the swinging light. Here the barges would swing around and face the way they have come, punching the tide and slowly dropping back to the piers at the entrance to Sharpness Docks. Most skippers made this look easy, but many a mate who fancied his chances at promotion, when handling the barge in between the piers for the first time, had second thoughts and

Above and opposite: *Four tanker barges lying on the mud at Sheperdine awaiting the next high tide.*

decided to forgo any thoughts of becoming master.

The unwritten law of who would enter Sharpness Lock first by vessels coming up the estuary was decided by which one arrived at the swinging light first. Sometimes a barge would try to push in, resulting in both vessels colliding and causing damage to each other. The management of the company did not condone this, but deemed the barge with the most damage as being the guilty one, even though it may not have been its fault!

Unlike the Bristol Channel ports, the lock at Sharpness only operates for a few hours on each tide, thus with many barges out in the river awaiting entry to the port, it was sometimes necessary to use the outer basin as a lock. This would cause a groan amongst the crews, as it would be quite a long time to fill the basin to the height of the main dock basin.

The Severn Estuary has witnessed many disasters over many years, with the majority taking place in the twentieth century. Did the men play a part in this, taking risks to gain that extra trip play a part in this, racing to be first at each port, ignoring nature and her powerful tides? Or were some barges just built with a jinx on them, as was the case with the *BP Explorer*, *Severn Carrier* and *Darleydale H*, all involved in more than one incident?

16 February 1961 – BP Explorer *Capsizes*

Fully laden to her winter load line, with 437 tons of petrol in the cargo tanks, the tanker barge *BP Explorer* left the confines of Swansea lock at 3.30 p.m. on 15 February 1961. Bound for Worcester, but with orders not to be there until the end of the week, her master, Capt. Harold Middleton, decided to sail to Barry Roads and anchor there until the following day.

Although this large tanker barge was owned by Shell-Mex & BP of London, she was managed by John Harker Ltd and crewed by their men. In fact there were another six similar vessels operating on the Severn and Bristol Channel, all managed by John Harker. They differed from other tanker barges working on the Severn in that they had a new revolutionary type of propeller. The 'Shell boats', as they were affectionately known, had fitted at the stern end a Voith-Schneider propulsion unit, which not only propelled the barge, but steered it as well. There were a series of vertical blades beneath the hull at the far stern end of the vessel and the action of them could be likened to someone sculling a boat with an oar.

The *BP Explorer* carried a crew of five men; skipper Harold Middleton (55), mate Ken Forster (39), engineer Alf Hook (39) plus two deckhands, Mike Holder (17) and Len Griffey (20). The extra deckhand was there to assist in the engine room, but normally the two young men would share these duties, both being competent seamen. When fully laden, these tanker barges were too deep to travel on the River Severn from Gloucester to Worcester, so they would stop at Gloucester to lighten their load by discharging 100 tons at Monk Meadow oil dock. In fact, in mid-1961 it was decided to stop operating the 'Shell boats' to Worcester due to the damage being done to the Voith-Schneider propulsion units. Because of the deep draft of the vessels, the blades were constantly being damaged by hitting the bed of the shallow river.

During 1962 Shell-Mex decided to convert one of the barges and fit a conventional propeller in place of the Voith-Schneider unit. They chose the *Shell Roadbuilder* and their crew was apprehensive as to whether it would improve the efficiency of the vessel. In deep water the Voith-Schneider unit performed well, the helmsman would sit at a console on the wheelhouse and steer the barge as he would his car. It would turn in her own length and go from ahead to astern immediately, unlike the famous 'Dale boats' of Harker's, which could be some swine to handle. There was no need to worry about the conversion of the *Shell Roadbuilder* though, she handled well and the crew were impressed.

At 7.15 p.m. the same day *BP Explorer* dropped anchor in Barry Roads after the uneventful trip up from Swansea. At Barry Roads ships bound for Sharpness and other ports in the Bristol Channel would anchor while awaiting tide or further orders. On Thursday 16 February the crew weighed anchor at 2.40 p.m. to slowly proceed with the flood tide towards Sharpness. High water there was at 9.00 p.m., which gave master Harold Middleton plenty of time to get there, especially as it was a large spring tide flowing that night. Three hours later they were off Avonmouth and about to enter the swirling waters of the Severn Estuary.

It was dark by then, but fine and clear with little wind. Out of Avonmouth came the little *Regent Wren*, another tanker barge, bound for Stourport. Between the *Regent Wren* and the *BP Explorer* was another tanker barge, the *Kendale H*, with skipper Jimmy Tonks at the wheel. All three vessels arrived at Slime Road, above Beachley, at about the same time, at about 6.30 p.m. The *Kendale H* was drawing 2ft less draft than the *BP Explorer* and before reaching Inward Rock, where he would turn across the Severn to the opposite bank, Tonks increased his speed. As he passed the *BP Explorer*, at a distance of 40ft, he gave a friendly wave to Middleton and received the same back. Mervyn Browning, engineer on the *Regent Wren*, who was at the helm, also passed the *BP Explorer*, but at a greater distance. They were 150ft apart, with the *BP Explorer* on Browning's port side.

Crossing the Severn here at the Counts Channel is tricky, the channel is relatively narrow and it is almost impossible for a helmsman to maintain a constant course. It takes great control of the vessel to keep her on a safe heading, as there is a violent turbulence, which sets up eddies within the main flow of the stream, which can be miniature maelstroms.

BP Explorer *crossing Swansea bay, empty, on her way towards Swansea Docks.*

The BP Explorer *berthed in Monk Meadow Dock, Gloucester.*

Jimmy Tonks saw the masthead light of *BP Explorer* turning into the Counts Channel as she altered course to come across the river, it was now two hours and forty minutes before high water at Sharpness. Mervyn Browning on the *Regent Wren* noticed, as he passed the tanker barge, cabin lights shining out through the portholes. Minutes later Tonks saw nothing; he did think though, that he could see an unlighted shape floating in the water.

Other craft had been bound for Sharpness on the evening tide including barges from Avonmouth and at least one other tanker barge from Swansea. Yet no one at Sharpness questioned why the *BP Explorer* had not docked on that tide! During that period vessels and ports rarely spoke to each other by radio, unless requesting assistance or to pass a message. It was not uncommon for masters of the tanker barges to radio each other giving out false information as to their location. Why? To lull a vessel bound for Swansea into thinking they would be first to load on arrival, only to find that as they approached the port someone had beaten

Why did the lock keepers at Sharpness not ask about the *BP Explorer*? Did they know she was bound for the port and had actually been on her way up the estuary? It was common practice that, as the last ship locked in or out on the tide, to lock the gates and be gone within minutes.

An eyewitness standing on the end of Lydney pier saw, at 8.20 p.m., an upturned vessel floating upstream on the strong flood tide which was estimated as running at between 5 and 6 knots. On the ebb tide the *BP Explorer* floated back down river, striking a column on the partly demolished Severn Railway Bridge with some force, and then grounding on Lydney Sands. them to the berth.

During low water at about 2.00 p.m. the following day, fireman and police went out across the sands to see if there were any of the crew still trapped in the upturned hull. They found no one inside.

That same day the body of skipper Harold Middleton was found washed ashore at Oldbury-on-Severn. All other four crewmen were officially classed as missing, presumed dead.

As the 400 tons of petrol leaked from the cargo tanks into the river, the smell of petrol fumes could be smelt for miles. Wreckage from the vessel began to be washed up onto the foreshore of the Severn; white rails and woodwork from the superstructure was found on the Lydney side of the Severn.

That Friday evening the tanker barge still seemed to be at the mercy of the tides, giving Sharpness harbourmaster, Capt. Burbage, cause for concern. He ordered men with search-lights on two vessels out in the Severn to keep track of the floating wreck. They lost her as she floated upstream again, bouncing through the Severn Railway Bridge.

The following day the *BP Explorer* was seen lying on the mud off Awre, a small village some six miles above Sharpness on the west bank of the Severn. The spring tides were by now dropping away, so the fear of her coming back down through the bridge again had diminished, but it had been considered a possibility to blow up the wreck where she lay embedded in the mud.

Firemen with breathing apparatus were now able to do a more detailed search of the vessel, but again nothing was found. Wire hawsers were strapped around the hull and secured to the shore to stop the wreck from floating again until plans were made as to what to do with her. The Metal Trading Co. of Swansea had been contracted to salvage the *BP Explorer* and were soon on the scene assessing the situation. By now all the cargo of petrol had leaked out into the river.

It was to take several weeks until all the missing bodies were found. A body was discovered at Alvington Pill on 9 March and was to be identified as that of the mate, Ken Forster.

The wreck of the BP Explorer *at Awre.*

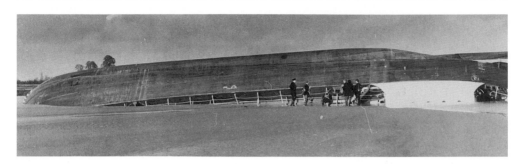

The starboard side of the upturned BP Explorer *at Awre.*

A naked body had been found in the estuary and was thought to have been that of Mike Holder, but unfortunately his father was unable to identify him, so he was buried at Thornbury in an unmarked grave. Later, when Mike's personal belongings were recovered from the *BP Explorer,* the body buried at Thornbury matched fingerprints on some of his possessions. Mike Holder's body was later exhumed on 20 April.

On Monday 11 April a salvage team at Awre were successful in righting the *BP Explorer.* For a number of days they had been winching the barge towards the bank on each high tide before righting her with a powerful hydraulic ram. After the tides had neaped, the barge was towed to Sharpness by the *Shell Glassmaker* (skipper, Tommy Carter) for rebuilding. Meanwhile all the sand and mud that had built up in the vessel was pumped out, which also enabled a more thorough search to be made of the tanker barge.

The upturned hull of the BP Explorer *at Awre.*

Firemen search the wreck of the BP Explorer *at Awre for missing crewmen.*

The BP Explorer *being searched for the bodies of the missing crewmen.*

Preparation for righting the hull of the BP Explorer.

Work begins to salvage the BP Explorer.

Following her rebuilding at Sharpness the vessel was renamed *BP Driver* and was to make headlines again on her third trip on the last day of January 1962.

At the Court of Inquiry held on 7 and 8 November 1961 at Gloucester, the reason for the capsizing of the *BP Explorer* was given as the vessel touching ground in such a manner and such speed as to produce an immediate reduction in positive stability and make her vulnerable to tidal forces, the precise magnitude and significance of which are impossible to determine.

The capsizing was not through any wrongful act or default by master, Harold Middleton, or any other crewmember.

BP Explorer

Motor Tanker Barge, built 1956, Official Number 187520.
Built By: W.J. Yarwood & Sons Ltd, Northwich.
Owned by: Shell-Mex & BP Ltd, London.
Managed by: John Harker Ltd.
303 grt, 139ft 3in long, 21ft 7in wide, 10ft 5in depth.
1961: Following the accident, salvaged and rebuilt at Sharpness Shipyard. Renamed *BP Driver*.

Crew of the *BP Explorer*

Skipper: Harold Middleton (55) of Longford Lane, Gloucester. Married with two daughters.
Mate: Ken Forster (39) of Matson Avenue, Gloucester. Married with two children.
Engineer: Alf Hook (39) of Beaufort Road, Gloucester. Married with three children.
Deckhand: Mike Holder (17) of Deans Way, Gloucester. Single man.
Deckhand: Len Griffey (20) of Baylands, Newtown, Berkeley. Single man.

31 January 1962 – BP Driver *Lost on the Nash*

Following her rebuild at Sharpness the *BP Explorer* was renamed *BP Driver* and began working again towards the end of 1961. The new crew of five men had to put all thoughts of that terrible night, almost a year previously when the vessel turned over in the Severn Estuary, behind them.

Two months into trading again the *BP Driver* left Sharpness bound for a routine trip, empty to Swansea, to load 470 tons of petrol for delivery to Worcester. Her crew now comprised the skipper Bill Merrett, a Severn tankerman of many years; mate Anthony Tatchell, who was new to the company; engineer James Storey; and deckhands Raymond Thomas and Ernest Sterry (on his first trip on the barge). It was a dark night as they passed Barry on their way down the Welsh coast to Swansea. Ahead of them lay the passage through the treacherous Nash Point, high cliffs on the starboard side and the Nash Sands on the port side. With just a narrow channel of turbulent water to get through this can be a daunting task, not for the faint-hearted.

As the *BP Driver* entered Nash Point at 8.30 p.m., guided in by the flashing light of the lighthouse 100ft above them, the fierce tide began to push the vessel close to the rocks. Bill Merrett, unable to hold his ship off into deeper water, felt her touch, first the shingle, then the jagged

The wreck of the BP Driver *on the rocks at The Nash.*

rocks. Capt. Merrett immediately sent out a Mayday call on his radio, which was received by the coastguards, and they in turn called out Barry lifeboat. Other vessels in the vicinity also picked up the Mayday call and proceeded to the area to see if they could be of assistance.

They arrived an hour later playing their searchlights onto the stricken vessel and surrounding rocks. The crew of five men could be seen clambering over the rocks to the safety of higher ground. Fortunately all escaped unhurt.

The lighthouse keeper above could see that the *BP Driver* was being pounded by high waves and was badly holed below the waterline.

Next day salvage experts and others surveyed the grounded *BP Driver* and found that it was not worth salvaging her. Still constantly battered by waves from the high tides their only option was to abandon her. A sad end to this unlucky vessel.

Crew of the *BP Driver*

Skipper: William Jonas Merrett of Randwick Road, Gloucester.
Mate: Anthony Tatchell of Cinderford Bridge, Cinderford.
Engineer: James Storey of Green Bank, Brockworth.
Deckhand: Raymond Thomas (17) of Hillview Road, Gloucester.
Deckhand: Ernest Sterry (16) of Coney Hill Road, Gloucester.

19 November 1961 – Man Lost from Launch

Construction of the Severn Bridge was progressing well and now the two towers either side of the Severn at Aust and Beachley could be seen rising from beneath the river. It was a remarkable feat of engineering to build a bridge across one of the most dangerous rivers in the world, especially as at this location the Severn has the second highest rise and fall of tide in the world. To put this into perspective, one has to see the river at low water level, then again at high water to note the vast difference. At low water a wide expanse of mud flats can be seen, yet on a high spring tide there can be as much as 40ft of water beneath the bridge. That is a lot of water to fill the estuary, especially as it rises in just over an hour, no wonder the Severn is dangerous.

HM Queen Elizabeth II officially opened the Severn Bridge on Thursday 8 September 1966. This was an exciting day for all those concerned in the building of the bridge, but marked the end of the Beachley-to-Aust ferry, which had been running across the river since *Enoch Williams* began the service on 6 July 1926. At the time this was classed as the new ferry, for there had been a ferry operating between these two hamlets since the eighteenth century. On 18 May 1931 the company, having been reformed, began a service with their new name of The Old Passage Severn Ferry Co. Ltd, the Beachley to Aust Ferry. Crossing the river here would save the motorist a fifty-five-mile detour via Gloucester, but was not without its risks! It was not unknown for a car to slip off the jetty as it was negotiating the difficult manoeuvre of getting onto the ferry, and slide into the Severn, thankfully, though, never with a loss of life.

The one day that men from the tanker barges least enjoyed leaving home on was a Sunday. This Sunday was no exception, except that they were to leave Gloucester at midday to make Sharpness in time for tide at about 6.00 p.m. Both the *Wyesdale H* and *Wharfedale H* left their berth at Monk Meadow, Gloucester, to begin the slow journey down the ship canal, one bound for Swansea, the other to Avonmouth. The weather was grey, but dry and quite mild for the time of year. Both barges arrived at Sharpness after an uneventful trip down the canal and waited to be called into the lock, then to begin the trip to their various ports.

As the two barges made their way down the estuary in darkness, drama was about to unfold in the Severn off Beachley. Three men working for the construction company John Howard & Co. were launching a small boat to row out to the bridge foundations. They began rowing from the shore when suddenly they were swept upstream by the powerful rising tide. Soon the little boat was swamped, leaving the men fighting for their lives in the strong currents of the river. Somehow the alarm was raised, heard luckily by the skipper of the Beachley-to-Aust ferry, *Severn Princess*, who was making his last trip of the day. Skipper Percy Palmer went in search, fearing the worst, but soon they had located one man, over towards Littleton-on-Severn, clinging to the upturned boat. Soon they had found the other two men, a further one and a half miles upstream, one of them, weighing seventeen stone, supporting his colleague in the water. On hearing the distress call, the construction company launched their launch *Isobella* at Chepstow and proceeded down the River Wye towards the Severn. Skipper of the motor launch, John Hollins of Chepstow, had just received a radio message informing him that the three missing men had been picked up by the ferryboat and on hearing this decided to swing his vessel around in the Severn Estuary and head back to Chepstow.

Meanwhile the two tanker barges, *Wyesdale H* and *Wharfedale H*, owned by John Harker Ltd, were well down the estuary from Sharpness. The two barges were lashed alongside one another, thus needing only one man to steer them, a practise frowned upon, but carried out from time to time. The skipper of the *Wharfedale H*, John Tonks, went aboard the *Wyesdale H* to steer both vessels, whilst both crews mingled with each other down in the cabins. The *Wharfedale H* was bound for Avonmouth, an old vessel with the cabin situated at the forward end for the crew of four men. The *Wyesdale H* skipper, George Thompson, was bound for Swansea. Although also with a crew of four men, she had far better accommodation, located aft, with each man having his own cabin. Chris Witts, deckhand on the *Wyesdale H*, took this opportunity to go aboard the *Wharfedale H* to chat to the crew.

Although dry, it was a dark night due to the cloud cover and as the *Isobella* entered the Severn below the Severn Bridge the skipper failed to see the two tanker barges coming down on the ebb tide from Slime Road towards the bridge. The mate on the *Isobella*, John Newton of Goldcliff, Newport, suddenly saw the two barges looming down towards them and screamed to his skipper to go full astern. In the darkness, with no navigation lights showing from the motor launch, Johnny Tonks on the *Wyesdale H* also failed to see the boat, not realising they were both on a collision course. To make it more difficult for Johnny Tonks, both tanker barges were empty and high out of the water, restricting his view over the bow. As they collided, the crew of the *Wharfedale H*, down in the forward cabin, heard a crashing sound, likened to chains rattling. Rushing up on deck they expected to see that they had hit the navigation lights marking the channel through the notorious Shoots.

They were shocked to see that a large motor launch had been cut in two and now lay between the two tanker barges, with one man stood on the wreckage shouting that his mate was in the water. The man was hauled to safety onto one of the tanker barges before both

The Rosedale H *lying on the mud at Sheperdine awaiting the next high tide.*

crews rejoined their respective vessels. Searchlights were played on the river and the missing man could be seen floating in the water shouting for help, but before they could get to him he had slipped beneath the waves. A distress call was made and it didn't seem long before the large, old lifeboat from Weston-super-Mare was on the scene. Named *Fifi and Charles*, this was to be her last call-out as a lifeboat before being replaced with a more modern vessel.

All three vessels circled around the scene trying desperately to locate the missing man, John Newton, but as the tide was by now ebbing away fast they had to quickly make for Avonmouth. All crewmen were tinged with sadness as they approached the piers at the entrance to the docks, to see ambulances and police waiting for them.

It was ironic that the boat sent out to rescue the three missing men should be involved in a separate incident of its own. John Hollins later said that he did see a red light shortly before the collision, but had assumed it was from a car's rear light on the shore at Beachley. This red light would have been the port navigation light of one of the two tanker barges. The body of John Newton was never found, like so many others who have fallen into the Severn.

Once they were locked in at Sharpness, the tanker barges loaded with petrol were not allowed to moor in the docks. Unlike the black-oilers, they had to proceed through the low-level bridge, under the high-level bridge, and tie up inside the entrance to the old dock from the canal. Then at 5.00 a.m. they would slip quietly away to begin the sixteen-mile trip along the Gloucester & Sharpness Ship Canal to Gloucester. Three hours later they would be passing through Llanthony Bridge into Gloucester Docks and heading across the dock basin towards the small lock where the barges, one at a time, would be lowered down to the level of the River Severn.

This lock and the one at Worcester governed the size of the tanker barges built during the 1950s and 60s. Barges such as the *Winsdale H* were 140ft long and almost 22ft wide and it would be a tight fit in these two locks. Great care had to be taken whilst going into Gloucester Lock from the dock basin, as nature would take over should the skipper get it wrong. If he was going too fast as the bow of the vessel entered the lock, the water displaced would come out of the lock, swirl around and then push the barge hard towards the outer gates. Going hard astern on the propeller had no effect on stopping the barge!

As soon as those outer gates opened the troubles would begin for the crew. There is a nasty current going across Gloucester Lock, from the quay wall down towards Llanthony Weir, and if care was not taken as the barge left the lock it could be taken down with the current towards the weir! It was common for the large tanker barges to have a check rope from the bow to the shore, carried by the lock-keeper until the vessel was about half way along the quay. Should the bow of the barge veer off across the river with the strong current the lock-keeper would place the eye of the rope onto a bollard as the crewmen briefly took a turn on their bollard to check the barge and keep them on a straight course. Sometimes the rope would break!

One incident reported by the local newspaper happened in 1962 when the small *Huntdale H* came out of Gloucester Lock loaded and bound for Stourport. These small barges very rarely used a check rope along the quay as they had sufficient depth of water underneath them to quickly gain enough speed to overcome the current across the lock entrance. But with the river low, the little *Huntdale H* was taken with the current across the channel adjacent to the lock.

The only way of getting her moved was to pump part of her cargo into another empty barge, which would hopefully assist in moving her into deeper water. The large *Rosedale H* was lying empty in Gloucester Docks with the crew stood by awaiting orders. They were instructed to lock out into the river and have part of the cargo from the *Huntdale H* pumped into their cargo tanks, then tow the small tanker barge onto the quay to have the cargo pumped back into her tanks.

Whilst this was happening a young lady had jumped into the Severn from Westgate Bridge, just around the bend from the quay, and drowned. Skipper of the *Rosedale H*, George Thompson, saw a young rookie policeman waiting with a grappling hook on the side of the quay waiting for her body to float down with the current. Taking his deckhand, Chris Witts, with him, he told the constable that they would get the young lady out of the river! The young deckhand did not find it a pleasant sight as they pulled the woman up the steps and onto the grass alongside the quay, not pleasant for the young constable either!

Three miles above Gloucester at Sandhurst the Severn splits into two channels, this section is called The Parting, with the East Channel for navigation and the West Channel running under the low Maisemore Bridge, with a weir a little way upstream. The East Channel is very narrow with a series of tight bends to negotiate, with the added problem of being quite shallow due to silt being deposited on the bed after the fortnightly spring tides.

The first large tanker barge to take her load to Worcester had serious problems in travelling up The Parting for the first time. She left Gloucester at 5.30 a.m., but by midnight had only travelled two miles! The crew persevered, though, and as other large tanker barges of the fleet joined her, the channel was slowly opened, but then only to bring new problems to the river. Over a long period of time the Severn has changed, but never so dramatically as within the last fifty years. Now the river is overgrown with trees and vegetation along both banks, along The Parting, in places, the trees actually touch each other across the water. Fifty years ago the banks were open, no trees to fall in the river, to become stuck on the bed and cause problems to passing craft. The channel was deep, free of silt as the large barges kept the depth of the river to 10ft; two tanker barges could even pass each other in the narrow width of The Parting.

21 September 1953 – Stuck Across the River

The tanker barge *Darleydale H* locked out of Gloucester Lock at midday bound for Worcester with a cargo of petrol. Built in 1937 she carried a crew of four men and traded between Avonmouth and Worcester. Although built with a large cargo-carrying capacity, her accommodation was basic, just one cabin located up in the bows, nothing like the standard of the similar sized 'Dale' boats of the 1950s.

It was shortly after 1.00 p.m. as she slowly made her way up the East Channel of The Parting towards the large house, known as The Jolly Waterman at Walham, once a favourite pub on the riverbank, that the *Darleydale H* lost her propeller. The tanker barge drifted back with the current and as the stern touched the bank her bow swung round and the vessel became jammed across the river. This is the worst scenario that a barge can find herself in, for the fast flowing current will push against the side of the vessel, which acts as a dam across the river.

A second tanker barge came upon the scene and began to give assistance in trying to pull the *Darleydale H* around, but only succeeded in getting herself stuck! Soon after this a third barge came to their assistance, but that too got wedged between both barges. Later that afternoon in driving rain and high winds all three vessels were stuck solidly across the river and there they lay until the next set of spring tides a week later.

The large spring tides rise up over the weirs of Llanthony and Maisemore, reversing the flow of the current as the great volume of water races towards Tewkesbury. Loaded barges would take advantage of this, reducing the trip time dramatically, but not without danger and excitement. Normally the place where the two opposing currents meet is below the Globe Inn, the first sign to the bargeman is when the bow of his barge drops to the riverbed, then rises up like a large whale. Soon they are racing up towards the Tar Works, where East Channel meets West, across a giant whirlpool, the barge being taken close into the right bank, adrenalin pumping through the helmsman as he struggles to keep away from hitting anything. Then relief comes as they come clear of The Parting and they can then relax as the barge races with the flow of water, accompanied by floating trees and debris of all kind, including at time, animals.

The remainder of the trip to either Worcester or Stourport was normally uneventful. In summer it was a struggle with low water levels, the river shallow and the barge touching bottom, adding hours to the trip. Yet in winter the levels rose with fresh water coming down from the Welsh hills, creating a different problem for the crews. If the river was too high then the barges would have difficulty in getting under the numerous bridges between Stourport and Gloucester when coming back downriver empty. With ballast tanks full, wheelhouse dismantled and sometimes even the cargo tanks filled with water, the barges would shoot under the bridges as they came down the river with alacrity. No chance of stopping if the skipper had misjudged his calculations, creating sheer fear, as the bridge looms, making it look from the deck of the barge, as though she would not go through!

Worcester Bridge gave problems to many a skipper bringing his barge down from Stourport; he had to be brave, for the only way to get through the arch was at speed. The

The tanker barge Darleydale H *towing the loaded dumb barge* Arkendale H *up The Parting at Gloucester sometime before 1948.*

bow would dip as they entered the bridge with the stern rising up, and then as the bow went out the other side the stern would dip down to go under the arch. Of course it did not always go as smoothly as that, witness the damaged stonework around the arches as barges sometimes collided with the bridge. Many a barge would come out the other side of the bridge without the wheelhouse or ventilators!

Not all bargemen were brave enough to shoot under the bridge in this fashion. Some would swing around and drop through the bridge stern first with the help of a rope from the shore or with the help of another barge. But this took time, something that was precious to tanker men.

20 December 1958 – Haw Bridge Disaster

Haw Bridge at Tirley, another difficult bridge to navigate under when the river is high, once featured in a national murder enquiry, now known as 'The Haw Bridge Torso Murder', but more about that later. A bridge was first built here in 1825, not designed by Thomas Telford as many think, although he did have an influence on where it was to be located. In those days there was great rivalry between Gloucester and Cheltenham, especially as to the route of any new road being built, as roads formed an important part in the trade of any town.

Telford had been asked to construct a road from Northleach to Milford Haven and he recommended it should pass through Cheltenham and Gloucester to cross the Severn at Over. Of course Cheltenham welcomed this plan, but thought that it was not in their interest for it to pass through Gloucester.

They put forward an alternative plan for the road to cross the Severn at Tirley, already the site of a ferry, which would then bypass Gloucester. The townsfolk of Cheltenham were so keen on this idea that a fund was started and soon there was enough money to build a bridge across the river at Haw Passage. In a very short time £19,000 had been collected, more than the original estimate of £17,925 required to construct a bridge.

By the time the bridge was opened in September 1825 the final cost of building the bridge and improving the local roads had risen to £24,348. Yet there was to be further bad news; Thomas Telford's original plan to cross the river at Over was accepted, including building his now famous Over Bridge at Gloucester.

This was terrible news for the people of Cheltenham, as Haw Bridge became a white elephant with even local people refusing to use it. They objected to the high toll charges and preferred to cross the Severn by way of the ferry. Local character Squire Hawkins is reputed to have swum across the river on horseback rather than pay the toll.

The bridge was built of two cast iron arches spanning the Severn supported by two large stone piers in the river. Always considered to be one of the more difficult bridges to pass under in times of flooding by the large tanker barges, as there was less air draught than on the other bridges they had to negotiate. Air draught being the distance between the underside of the bridge and the river.

The John Harker tanker barge *Darleydale H* had left Gloucester at 5.00 a.m. on Saturday 20 December 1958 for a routine return trip to Worcester, with the crew expecting to be back in its hometown later that night. The Severn was running high with 7ft of freshwater above

21 December 1958 at Haw Bridge, showing the Darleydale H *moored to the bank of the River Severn.*

normal level, not too much though for the skipper, Stanley Edwards of Chepstow, to worry about. Although the *Darleydale H* had a large cargo-carrying capacity, she was an old tanker barge, built for a crew of four men, but with a cabin located at the forward end in the bow, and because of this the vessel only traded between Avonmouth and Worcester.

On completion of pumping out her cargo, the *Darleydale H* was eased gently astern out of the oil basin at Diglis in Worcester into the fast flowing current of the River Severn, then locking through Diglis Lock before settling down for the run back to Gloucester. Soon it would be dark and the only aid they had to navigate the Severn in darkness would be a pair of car headlights fixed to the bow! All that could hope to be illuminated would be the bank on either side, slightly ahead of the barge.

Having passed through Upper Lode Lock at Tewkesbury the mate of the *Darleydale H*, John Rickards of Matson, Gloucester, took the wheel and steered the vessel on down towards Gloucester. It had been raining that day with a strong fresh wind, but as they passed Deerhurst on the left bank the rain stopped and the night became quite clear. It was about 5.30 p.m. as they approached the 'S' bend, with a final left turn towards Haw Bridge, when the skipper ordered John Rickards to go forward to shine the lights onto the bridge as they went through. Engineer, Gerald Sullivan of Gloucester, also went forward to assist the mate and they were stood at the highest point of the vessel as the bows passed under the bridge. It is quite frightening approaching Haw Bridge when the river is in flood, when standing on a large tanker barge thinking she will not go under. Both men ducked, as all crewmen instinctively do, and then heard a thud and a crash.

The tanker barge began to roll and as they looked aft could see that part of the bridge had fallen onto their vessel. As they ran back aft they could hear Stan Edwards shouting, 'Come and free me'. The barge was still going ahead fast and suddenly struck the right bank so heavily that it threw Rickards to the deck, then slewed around in the river and began to head upstream back to the bridge. It was about this time that the second span of the bridge fell into the river.

Gerry Sullivan managed to get to the engine controls to shut the engine down and then went to the wheelhouse where he found the skipper lying beneath debris and heavy metal girders from the bridge.

A young lad on the shore that night, thirteen-year-old Kenneth Jones of Tirley, said he had seen the tanker barge coming down the river with her lights high out of the water. He followed it down towards Haw Bridge expecting it to swing around and go back upstream, as she was too high to go under the bridge. He saw the bows of the *Darleydale H* going under the bridge with a man crouching down holding the headlights, then the stern slewed around towards where he was standing on the Ledbury side of the river. Young Jones did not see the collision, but saw part of the bridge dropping down onto the barge.

As he cycled home to tell his father, he heard the other span dropping into the river. Then together they went back to the scene of the disaster to warn road traffic of the danger. Another local man, water bailiff Phillip Gaskin, was soon told of the accident and took his punt out onto the river and rowed down to the *Darleydale H*. He helped the crew anchor the vessel before assisting them with the release of the skipper from beneath the debris.

An ambulance was called from Tewkesbury and the two attendants had to wade through mud before Phillips Gaskin was able to ferry them to the *Darleydale H*. Massive iron girders had to be levered away from the skipper before they were able to get him onto a stretcher and into the punt to return to the ambulance. Stan Edwards was taken to Cheltenham General Hospital where he was certified dead.

The damaged Darleydale H *towed down the River Severn after hitting Haw Bridge.*

The damaged Haw Bridge after the tanker barge Darleydale H *had knocked it down.*

Two other small tanker barges were on their way down river that night bound for Gloucester, the first was the *Regent Jill*, skippered by Basil Lane who fortunately saw a police car on the bank above Haw Bridge flashing his headlights at him. Basil put the bows of his tanker barge into the left bank with the force of water swinging him around to face the current. Mooring to the bank, skipper Lane had to signal to the second barge coming down river to stop before rounding the last bend and hitting the bridge now lying across the river. He managed to attract the attention of the crew of the *Regent Swallow* in plenty of time for them to swing around and moor to a tree on the bank.

By 24 December the level of the Severn had dropped by 4ft, allowing small barges to pass through the demolished bridge. To keep the important supply of petroleum products getting to Worcester it was necessary to clear a wide channel through the bridge for the large tanker barges to get through. Hundreds of people watched on 29 December as a large crane lifted part of the iron bridge out of the Severn.

The inquest into the death of Stan Edwards was held at Cheltenham on Wednesday 14 January 1959, but the vital question as to what wrecked Haw Bridge remained unanswered. Two suggestions were put forward, one saying that the bridge was mined during the Second World War and that the fuses were not removed and secondly that the *Darleydale H* had been pushed off course by the strong current and hit the bridge. The first suggestion was ruled out by the County Surveyor.

The Coroner, Mr J.D. Lane, said that Stan Edwards had died as a result of debris falling from the bridge and recorded a verdict of death by misadventure. It was thought that the steel decking from the pump house of the *Darleydale H* collided with the bridge as the tanker barge was passing under Haw Bridge. With plenty of freshwater coming down the Severn, a large barge coming around the last left hand bend has a tendency for the stern of the vessel to swing over to the right-hand side. If the stern is allowed to go over too much it would have been

The damaged Haw Bridge after the tanker barge Darleydale H *had knocked it down.*

difficult to straighten up before going through the bridge and as mentioned before, the original Haw Bridge was low with curved arches.

At a meeting of the Gloucestershire Highways Committee on 19 January plans to rebuild Haw Bridge were approved at a cost of £200,000, unfortunately it could be up to two years before the bridge would be open. Meanwhile it was agreed that soldiers from the Royal Monmouthshire Royal Engineers would construct a Bailey Bridge across the river at a cost of £7,500. Until the Bailey Bridge was open, Gloucestershire County Council agreed to allow pedestrians to cross the river on the ferry free of charge.

Friday 12 June 1959 was declared the day for the official opening of the Bailey Bridge with the band of the Royal Monmouthshire Regiment leading men and officers across the bridge. The Bailey bridge was in use for only two years, for on Saturday 30 September 1961 the new Haw Bridge was opened.

With the river in flood some barges would go over the weirs, and even the large ones would race across Upper Lode Weir at Tewkesbury, saving valuable time by not having to negotiate the locks. Then finally they would reach The Parting and more problems with sharp narrow bends to be got round, the racing current trying to throw the barge into the outside bank. There is only one way to overcome this. The speed of the barge must be slightly faster than the current and it is a frightening experience as the helmsman looks sideways to see the metal piling of the bank flashing by. If the manoeuvre is misjudged and the barge doesn't go around the bend, she will simply drop over to hit the bank and then run out of control to the next bend before stopping, becoming jammed across the river.

About half a mile upstream of Westgate Bridge at Gloucester, the railway line out of the city

An empty tanker barge negotiates the Haw Bridge during the floods of 1959. The collapsed structure was replaced temporarily by this Bailey Bridge following the accident of December 1958.

crosses the Severn en route to South Wales over Black Bridge, rebuilt about 1958, making life a lot easier for the men on the barges. Before 1958, if the Severn had a large amount of fresh water running down, the large Worcester tanker barges of John Harker Ltd would swing around in the river before entering the East Channel of The Parting. This manoeuvre allowed the skippers to take their barges through Black Bridge slower than the fast flowing current, but was not without problems. A skipper would put the bow of his vessel into the bank and let the current swing the stern around. From this point the engine was not used to take the barge astern into The Parting and on down the river to Gloucester, only to go ahead if the current was taking them down too fast, acting as a brake. To get around the sharp bends the anchor was dropped, which could be tiresome, or, as some did, put a wire hawser around the anchor stock to hold it above the water and then let the heavy chain drag along the bottom.

The rounding of the last bend before the quay at Gloucester should have been a relief for the crews, but here the current is exceptionally fast as it flows around the bend at Gloucester Lock before running over the weir only a couple of hundred yards ahead. A barge coming onto the quay stern first with the river full of fresh water has not a great deal of control, as the skipper of the *Wandale H* found to his cost one day! The stern of the vessel touched the quay wall, but the bow was too far out into the river. Too late, the fast flowing river swung the barge around with the stern touching the bank on the opposite side of the river and the bow heading for the wall by the lock-keeper's cottage. They ended up across the Severn below the lock, pinned tightly to both banks by the current, not able to move without assistance. All ballast had to be pumped out and with the help of a local tug were eventually pulled back towards Gloucester Lock.

17 February 1958 – Steel Plates Ripped Open

There was plenty of fresh water running down the river and the tanker barge *Westerndale H* had left Worcester early in the morning, empty, bound for Gloucester. With the level of the Severn rising quite rapidly her skipper, Albert Tonks, thought it wise to fill some of the cargo tanks with water to help ballast the vessel down.

At 10.00 a.m. the *Westerndale H* had entered The Parting and was rounding the bend before Black Bridge when misfortune occurred. The original Black Bridge was built to carry the South Wales railway line out of Gloucester and was the lowest bridge across the Severn below Worcester. Albert Tonks carefully positioned his barge in the river ready to negotiate the difficult S bend; one error and the vessel would crash into the bank and become uncontrollable. Unfortunately this is what happened and the strong current swept the barge into the piling beneath the railway bridge. A large gash was ripped in the hull on the starboard side, quickly filling the engine room with water, which in turn stopped the engine.

As the *Westerndale H* drifted helplessly down river the crew fought to regain control of her. Tonks was fighting with the wheel as he rounded the last bend before Gloucester Lock when he saw the *Wyesdale H* coming towards him. Skipper of the *Wyesdale H*, George Sunderland, realising the plight that Albert Tonks was in, ploughed his way upstream from the lock in an endeavour to get a rope aboard the stricken tanker barge to bring her under control.

A rope was got aboard, but it parted before control could be regained. There was only one thing left to do, with only seconds in which to do it. That was to nose the bow of the *Westerndale H* onto the quay wall, then to quickly make her fast with ropes before she ran the risk of missing the lock entrance and coming to grief across Llanthony Weir. To the relief of both skippers, this was achieved and all that remained was to work the *Westerndale H* into Gloucester Lock with ropes, then a spell in the local shipyard to have the damage repaired.

Getting a large tanker barge into Gloucester Lock was difficult, with only a spare inch either side of the vessel and the strong current across the entrance giving skippers little room for error. As is the case when coming out loaded, a check rope is needed, this time the lad had to jump off the barge at the top end of the quay and walk along with the eye of the rope, ready to drop it onto a bollard. The mate would then take a turn on his bollard to line up the bow with the entrance to the lock, the skipper back aft in the wheelhouse hoping that the rope would not break. The chunks taken out of the stonework to the entrance of the lock prove that the rope broke on many an occasion!

Chapter Six
Rescue and Pilots

Severn Area Rescue Association

The River Severn has many natural hazards between Avonmouth and Gloucester, especially in the tidal estuary. Below the entrance to the River Wye is an area known as The Shoots, rocks and sand covered about three hours before high water, presenting a vicious tidal race. Above here are wide areas of shifting mud and sandbars, where the river runs through the main channel at a speed in excess of 10 knots, with the water level rising to over 30ft in two hours. With numerous accidents taking place on this treacherous stretch of the Severn many local people were concerned that no rescue boat was available to assist anyone in trouble.

During the early part of the 1970s the RNLI was approached and asked if it could provide a Rescue Station, but it was discovered that RNLI boats do not operate in estuarine waters. The nearest RNLI Station was at Penarth in South Wales, twenty-five miles away in the Bristol Channel and too far to come to assist someone in difficulty in the estuary. In 1973 SARA (Severn Area Rescue Association) was formed to provide a rescue boat for the tidal estuary of the River Severn, but did not become operational until 1976. In those early days their base was at a lock-up garage in the garden of a house in Tutshill, near Chepstow, before establishing a new Station in 1993 under the Severn Bridge at the head of the slipway at Beachley.

SARA is unique in that it also provides a Mountain Rescue Team who, together with the Fire Service Cliff Rescue Team and Ambulance personnel, regularly rescue climbers trapped at Symonds Yat Rock and Wintours Leap. Injured climbers are taken in the inshore rescue boat down the River Wye to a landing point at Chepstow Bridge or to their slipway at Beachley.

Due to an increasing number of calls being received from above Sharpness it was decided in 1986 to open a second station close to the docks. Now that station is located in what was once the Harbourmaster's house at the Old Sharpness Docks, officially opened by the well-known television naturalist, Johnny Morris.

There are four rescue boats in the fleet, all equipped with the latest communications equipment, plus vehicles to tow the boats above the tide. The men are highly trained with regular exercises on the Severn, sometimes involving helicopters of the Royal Navy and RAF, who will spend a weekend in the area working with both the lifeboat men and Cliff Rescue Team.

Like the RNLI, SARA is also a charity and relies on public support to provide this valuable rescue service on the Severn and Wye. It is not unusual to see the men and their families at different events around the counties with a lifeboat, demonstrating their skills and at the same time seeking public support.

Both SARA Stations attend on average about sixty calls a year, varying from people trapped by the incoming tide to ships in difficulty. Some examples include the following:

Four people and a ten stone dog stuck in the mud in the River Wye.

Windsurfer in difficulty off Sheperdine.
Climber having fallen from the Devil's Pulpit at Shorncliff. Airlifted to hospital.
Assisting during the November 2000 flooding at Gloucester.

Monday 20 May 1996 – Sailing Ship Runs Aground

The 100ft long Sail Training Ship *Royalist* had spent a few days in Gloucester Docks having completed a training course for forty sea cadets from all over the UK. This magnificent two-masted brigantine was in Gloucester as part of the 75th anniversary celebrations for the Gloucester sea cadets and had been open to the public during the weekend.

From Gloucester the *Royalist* sailed down the canal to Sharpness, bound for the Festival of the Sea at Bristol. Hired by a private company, she was carrying passengers and an experienced crew, all looking forward to seeing many more tall ships gathered together at Bristol. Shortly before midday the brigantine left Sharpness, having taken on board the obligatory estuary pilot and in perfect sunshine rounded the piers to sail down the Severn on the ebbing tide.

Then at precisely 12.35 p.m. a coxswain from SARA received a phone call from one of his neighbours to say the *Royalist* was in trouble in the Severn. From where he lived he could see the ship aground down by the Counts Buoy with a 40-45 degree list to port and abeam to a fast flowing ebbing tide. First he rang HM Coastguard to report the incident, and then in some haste, joined his colleagues at the SARA Station at Beachley.

SARA 1 sped up the estuary towards the stricken ship, where it soon became clear that the *Royalist* was hard aground on the Narlwood Rocks. As the lifeboat came close to the brigantine, verbal contact was made with the crew who confirmed that all on board were safe and there were no causalities. Then suddenly from the blind side of the ship the lifeboatmen were horrified to see that an inflatable boat had been launched with six persons on board and in the fast flowing current they were being taken down onto the rocks. Seconds before hitting the rocks the outboard engine was raised, leaving them no choice but to paddle their way off into deeper water. The crew of *SARA 1* became concerned for their safety, but were unable to get close without going aground themselves, so shouted to them with instructions of where to go into deeper water.

The rescuers were amazed to see that of the six in the inflatable, five were women, one of them five months pregnant! A decision was made to take the pregnant woman and three of the others to the slipway at Beachley where a waiting paramedic could attend to her. The two remaining in the small inflatable were instructed not to return to their ship.

Meanwhile HM Coastguard had scrambled an RAF rescue helicopter from Chivenor, *SARA 2* from Sharpness and an RNLI inshore rescue boat, which had been in the Avonmouth area. As *SARA 1* returned to the scene, the men could see the RAF helicopter landing on the flat top of Narlwood Rocks and taking passengers on board from the brigantine. Two more rescue craft arrived, the *SARA 3* from Beachley and the *SARA 4* from Sharpness, all able to assist with laying out anchors ready for the evening tide.

The weather had taken a turn for the worse and with heavy rain and a strong wind all they could do now was to wait in anticipation for the incoming tide. As the tide reached the *Royalist*, the ship slowly slid from the flat surface of the rock into deeper water with a fear that she may roll completely onto her opposite side. This did not happen and the anchors held her in position until the engine was started and on the ebb tide the *Royalist* continued the trip down the estuary to Avonmouth.

Gloucester Harbour Trustees

Engaging the services of a pilot to navigate a ship into ports around the world is nothing new. Local men would offer their knowledge to merchantmen to sail ships through sometimes complicated channels, avoiding rocks and sandbanks. This knowledge would be passed from father to son, in small communities, creating family dynasties. One such community existed at Crewkerne Pill on the west bank of the River Avon, near Bristol. From here the pilots would sail in their fast Bristol Channel cutters down the channel and out into Western Approaches, sailing in dangerous waters with no guarantee of a ship to pilot home. Self-employed, these pilots would employ a professional seaman and a boy apprentice to sail the cutter back to their berth in the River Avon after he had boarded a ship to take safely back up the Bristol Channel.

It was not until 1861 that navigation of the Bristol Channel and River Severn was placed in the hands of the Pilots of the Port of Bristol; the pilots were then required to be licensed and abide by certain new Acts of Parliament. With its fierce tides the Severn posed a threat to pilots and masters alike, both refusing to sail up the estuary during dark winter nights. In 1888 eight beacons were erected in the Severn estuary, but only lit between September and May of each year, as no revenue from ship owners was collected to help pay for their maintenance. By 1890 the Sharpness Lighthouse Trustees was formed and began to levy dues on vessels trading along the estuary. Later that year the Gloucester Harbour trustees were constituted and now their area of operation is seaward of the Second Severn Crossing, to include the tidal reaches of the River Wye to Bigsweir Bridge and of the River Severn to both weirs at Llanthony and Maisemore at Gloucester. Ships bound for Sharpness pick up the estuary pilot at Barry, their job not complete until their ship is safely in the lock at that Port.

Besides supplying pilots for ships trading to the Severn Estuary, Gloucester Harbour Trustees have to maintain a safe navigation channel and to maintain the navigational aids within that channel. Many vessels have foundered in the estuary, some causing problems for the Trustees in getting the wrecks removed from the navigational channel. Some of these incidents are worthy of note as shown by the sailing ship *Prince Victor*.

April 1887 – Prince Victor

Nowadays ships trading to Sharpness generally come from Europe, but incredibly, over a century ago, large sailing ships would sail into the Bristol Channel from all parts of the world, bound for this little Gloucestershire port.

One such ship was the *Prince Victor*, which had left New York on 5 March loaded with 10,000 casks of paraffin. A month later this magnificent sailing ship entered the Bristol Channel and sailed towards Avonmouth, where on 3 April she dropped anchor at the Kingroad anchorage to await a large tide to take her up to Sharpness.

Her Norwegian captain, Hans Cornelinsen, had on board his wife and two young sons and all were looking forward to visiting Sharpness for the first time. Because his ship was deeply laden to a draught of 21ft 5in he had to wait for five days before the spring tides would put sufficient water under his vessel to safely take the ship over the rocks and sand banks in the estuary.

On the Good Friday of 8 April Gloucester pilot, Henry Smart, came aboard shortly before 5.00 a.m. ready to navigate the *Prince Victor* up the tortuous channel to Sharpness. The pilot planned to arrive at Sharpness just before high water, which that day was predicted at 8.00 a.m., but sailing against a strong north easterly wind could add time to the trip. Capt. Cornelinsen left the navigation of his ship to the pilot, but still remained on deck throughout the passage up the Severn Estuary. Due to the narrow channel and the strong currents in the estuary, it was necessary for the sailing ship to be assisted by three steam tugs: the *Ranger* of Gloucester, the *Refuge* of Cardiff and the *Victoria* of Newport. Both the *Ranger* and *Refuge* were towing the ship, while the *Victoria* lay alongside the port side of the vessel as the ship's pilot stood in the fore-castle of the *Prince Victor*, relaying instructions to the helmsman at the wheel.

The weather soon deteriorated, the wind increasing in strength as they passed Chapel Rock. At Lyde Rock pilot Henry Smart gave orders for the course to be altered to port, but as the tugs began to turn a sudden squall of wind prevented the ship from making the turn. The pilot began shouting more orders, but was not heard above the noise of the wind and soon the strong tide was setting the sailing ship down onto Whirl's End Sands, where she grounded and heeled over onto the tug *Victoria*. The *Victoria* cast off her ropes and was taken away by the tide before sinking a short distance away. Water poured into the accommodation of the *Prince Victor*, where Capt. Cornelinsen's wife, Nathalie, had been sheltering with her children. She, together with the younger son drowned, but fortunately the ship's steward rescued the eldest son. All other persons on the ship managed to take to the lifeboats before being picked up by the two bow tugs. It had been presumed that the crew of the sunken tug had been killed as she foundered, but miraculously they had managed to launch their lifeboat and sail away to safety.

With the tide still rising the *Prince Victor* became afloat again and drifted for four miles before grounding at Woolaston as the tide ebbed. There she lay, secured to the bank with mooring ropes as the masts and rigging were cut away, before some 400 tons of cargo were discharged into trows. A week later she was towed to Sharpness with the help of four tugs, to have the remainder of her cargo taken out of the hold.

The funeral of Nathalie Cornelinsen and her younger son took place on Wednesday 13 April at Woolaston Church, attended by the eighteen Norwegian crew members, who then returned home to Norway.

December 1906 – St Agnes

The ketch *St Agnes* was inward bound for Sharpness when suddenly the vessel sank in the channel opposite Inward Rocks. Realising that the ketch was a total wreck the owner abandoned the vessel, which then placed the responsibility for removing the obstruction with the Trustees.

The only way of clearing the obstruction was by dynamite, carried out in 1907 by a local salvage company. To recover some of the costs involved with the removal of the wreck the Trustees made a claim against the owner of the *St Agnes*, but these were never recovered. It was found that the owner of a stranded vessel was not liable if the value of the salvaged vessel would be less than the cost of the salvage! Once abandoned, any stranded vessel ceases to have an owner, making it the responsibility of the Trustees to carry out the necessary salvage work. This could have given them serious problems if a large vessel became wrecked in the estuary.

March 1945 – the John

A steamship, the *John*, fully laden with a cargo of coal was proceeding downriver when she became stranded and sank on the Gruggy Rocks, west of The Shoots. At high water all that could be seen were her masts and funnel, which gave tug skippers cause for concern and they refused to tow dumb barges down on the ebb tide when visibility was poor.

The owners of the *John*, A.J. Smith of Bristol, informed their underwriters and the Trustees of their intention to abandon the vessel as a total loss. The Trustees felt that the only way to remove the vessel was by dynamite, but were ordered not to do so because of the close proximity of the Severn Railway Tunnel. Nature gave a helping hand, though, for some large tides destroyed the wreck enough to prevent it becoming a danger to shipping.

February 1950 – William Ashburner

Whilst on passage up the estuary in thick fog on 1 February 1950, the motor schooner *William Ashburner* ran aground on Chapel Rock. Fortunately the pilot and crew were able to scramble ashore to safety.

On the following tide the schooner floated off the rocks at high water and was seen down off the mouth of the River Usk at Newport. It was not until the next tide that the *William Ashburner* floated back up the estuary and finally grounded in Slime Road!

Eventually the vessel came into the ownership of the Chepstow & District Yachting Club and was used in the training of local sea cadets. Sadly it was not long before the *William Ashburner* sank at the mouth of the River Wye, where today the hulk can be seen at low water.

December 1950 – Safety

The little motor barge *Safety* went aground in the river between the Fishinghouse Light and Hills Flats buoy which gave some concern to the Gloucester Harbour Trustees. They informed the barge owner, T. Silvey Ltd of Bristol, that they would be held responsible for any obstruction to navigation. Fortunately for the company the little *Safety* was refloated in January 1951 and taken to Bristol for repair.

April 1952 – Darleydale H

On the night tide of 4 April 1952 the tanker barge *Darleydale H* left Avonmouth bound for

Sharpness. With eight other craft they were passing Hills Flats buoy and approaching Hayward Rocks when the *Darleydale H* scraped over rocks beneath her. John Harker Ltd claimed that the buoy marking the rocks was not on station and subsequently made a claim for damages against the Trustees.

Hayward Buoy had broken away from its station on 25 March 1952 and after repairs was re-moored on 8 April 1952. No notice of the missing buoy had been issued to mariners, but Sharpness Harbourmaster had verbally informed pilots and masters of vessels alike.

The Trustees questioned the claim from John Harker Ltd, who now issued a writ to claim their damages of £550. At their annual meeting in April 1953 the Trustees considered the following points:

The provisions of the Harbour Order are permissive and not obligatory.

They estimated that the *Darleydale H* must have been considerably out of her normal course as Hayward Rocks is about 350ft distant from the centre of the channel with Conigre Lights in line. This suggested faulty navigation, as Hayward Rocks buoy is a marker buoy only and unlit at night. During the period that the buoy was off station a total of 186 craft had sailed through the channel including three large ships.

The master of the *Darleydale H* had taken his vessel through safely on five previous occasions when the buoy was off station.

Although the Trustees are responsible for the buoys in the Severn Estuary, which are there as an aid to navigation, vessels must still navigate with due care and attention.

The claim was contested, but in September 1954 was settled out of court with the Trustees having to pay a total of £474.

September 1958 – Lighter No.9

A tug towing lighters laden with logs for Lydney was approaching Berkeley Pill on 20 September 1958 when one of the lighters, Lighter No.9, sank. A week later Lighter No.9 was seen drifting on a flood tide towards Sharpness where again it sank! This time in a most awkward position, in between the Entrance Piers, right in the middle of the navigation channel.

The Trustees informed the lighter owner, F.A. Ashmead & Son Ltd of Bristol, that they were liable for the costs incurred in removing the wreck. £750 was claimed, but was contested by the company and eventually 90% of this sum was awarded to the Trustees.

November 1960 – Shinfield

Two years later the little tug, *Robert A*, was towing lighters on 4 November 1960 to Lydney when, again, one of them sank. Loaded with logs, the lighter *Shinfield* sank between the Upper Shoots Beacon and Charston Rock. The logs floated away from the lighter, but as the craft had sunk in deep water they did not pose a threat to shipping. The cargo of logs was later recovered, one by one, from the estuary.

These lighters were loaded deep in the water with the heavy logs open to the elements. No wonder then that several of them would sink whilst on passage up the Severn estuary to Lydney.

Chapter Seven

River Severn Floods

The River Severn begins her journey to the sea from high up in the Welsh hills of Plynlimon. Here an average of 2.3m of rain falls each year, compared to only 0.5m 220 miles away in the estuary. A lot of this rainfall at the source is absorbed into the land, the remainder running down the slopes into the river, where soon tributaries join it, making the Severn deeper and wider as it carries the extra water towards Gloucester.

The Severn will soon flood if a large amount of rainfall falls in a short space of time, with the ground becoming saturated and unable to absorb more water. Some of the more serious floods have been the result of a rapid thaw melting large amount of snow and ice in Wales, sending torrents of water down the river. Another cause, but more rare, has been a tidal surge from the Atlantic into the Bristol Channel and Severn Estuary.

The Environment Agency now issue regular flood warnings on all rivers in the UK, but this is a fairly new idea and up until recently people living alongside the Severn were expected to know what to expect! Residents knew the signs of an impending flood and would prepare their homes accordingly, light furniture moved upstairs, carpets taken up and plenty of sandbags at the ready.

It is difficult to predict what precisely will happen during the flood. Many factors make it complicated as nature has a mind of her own, but when the water begins to enter the home, misery begins. As a general rule should the Severn rise quickly, then levels will drop back down as quick, but a slow rise in levels usually means the floods could be with us for weeks.

Some residents have lived alongside the Severn all their lives and being flooded is just another annual event. They are well prepared, with electric sockets fitted well above ground level, no fitted carpets and a good stock of tinned food. The problems can increase as the water subsides, but again some are well prepared. With the garden hose at the ready, as soon as the last bit of water vanishes out through the front door the walls and stone floor are being washed with fresh water, taking away the silt and smells.

Sadly some floods have caused death and destruction and will continue to do so as long as the Severn floods. For centuries people have tried to prevent flooding from the river by building defences to stop the water topping over the bank into surrounding properties. Unfortunately one man's flood defence is another man's flood, as the water has to go somewhere!

October 1483 – The Duke of Buckingham's Water

During the second year of King Richard III's reign the Duke of Buckingham was advancing with his army from the Forest of Dean towards Gloucester. The army had been marching for a while and were becoming exhausted, so the Duke planned to cross the Severn at Gloucester before taking a rest in the city.

As the men rested between the city and the river a great flood came up the Severn, the depth so great that it surged over the banks drowning the men in their beds. Children in cradles were carried with the water across fields together with animals, including horses from the Duke's army.

The flood continued for ten days and is remembered as 'The Duke of Buckingham's Water'.

Tuesday 20 January 1606 – Riches to Rags

Rain had been falling for many days, the Severn above Gloucester had a lot of fresh water coming down from the Welsh hills and the tides were running high in the estuary. As was normal in the seventeenth century, people who worked the land in the country did not rise from their beds in winter until daylight. This day was no exception, especially as it was cold outside, with a strong wind and rain making it unpleasant to be out in the elements.

As the spring tide rolled in from the Atlantic, people along both sides of the Bristol Channel were alarmed to see the waters rising very quickly. In Gloucestershire, in the villages of Saul and Arlingham, farm workers and others still lay in their beds as this great mass of water surged up the estuary and across the land. It was 9.00 a.m. as people looked out of their windows to see what they thought was a mist across the land, not realising what danger they were in. In less than five hours water covered the land either side of the estuary and many hundreds of men, women and children perished in the flood.

Both sides of the Severn were covered by water for a distance of six miles inland. It is estimated that 500 people perished that day, besides thousands of animals, including cattle, sheep and pigs. Many people rich in the morning were paupers by the afternoon. One eyewitness said it was a strange sight to see the carcasses of wild animals, foxes, rabbits, rats, etc., floating together with dead people and cattle.

The salt water rose to a level of 7ft across the land and those people lucky enough to have climbed onto the roofs of their houses were rescued by rowing boats.

It is now thought that this tidal surge, on the highest tide of the year, was caused by an earthquake somewhere out in the Atlantic. On checking previous records it seems that this great tidal surge occurs about every 200 years!

The famous Severn Bore is formed twice a month during the spring tides, due to the lunar cycle. The Atlantic Ocean is so powerful that during these spring tides it pushes the tide, with some force, into the Bristol Channel, which narrows from its wide mouth like a funnel. Because the water is being compressed, the leading waves begin to rise and gain some speed, especially as it enters the Severn Estuary. On reaching Epney the tide has peaked and in fact is beginning to ebb at Sharpness, yet the water still races on up the river to Gloucester and beyond!

A little below Epney on the opposite bank is the large village of Newnham-on-Severn. Here the river has claimed many lives as the tide races by, as it did in 1731 when a trow struck the sands above Amity Crib. The tide swept over them drowning the owner and seventeen passengers, with four escaping in a small boat.

The reason why it is called a spring tide, is that it is like a coiled spring when compressed and then released, it pushes the water on as the tide ebbs. Some five miles below Gloucester the river narrows quite considerably, forcing the leading wave up to a height of 6ft and causing it to travel at over 10mph, creating the Severn Bore.

The wave is stopped at Gloucester due to the two weirs of Llanthony and Maisemore, yet the flow rises over them and travels on to Tewkesbury. Here the weir at Upper Lode stops the flow, but for about five minutes the level at the lock is the same top and bottom, allowing all lock gates to be open at the same time!

November 1770 – Gloucester Flooded

Should the river above Gloucester be full with fresh water this can have serious consequences for the city during the spring tides. The tides, as they race towards the city, hold back the current coming downriver, causing the water to rise over the banks and flood the surrounding area.

The last thirty years of the eighteenth century saw much rain falling over England and Wales making life a misery for those living near the Severn. Towns in England and Wales were suffering flooding on a regular basis, and whilst one region would have a serious flood, elsewhere it may not be so bad.

Gloucester had seen continual heavy rain and its populace became worried as the river rose, as a large tide was due on Thursday 19 November 1770. The tide came as predicted and held back the current coming downstream until it flowed over the banks and began to rise up into Westgate Street. Inhabitants were forced to leave their homes as St Mary's Square became flooded to a depth of 3ft. The mail from Worcester and South Wales did not arrive until the Sunday and had to be ferried by boat to those who chose to remain in their homes.

So badly was the city affected that an emergency meeting was arranged with the Mayor to consider how they could help to relieve the distress of the poor who were exposed to this dreadful flood.

By Thursday 26 November 1770 the flood began to recede, although meadows were still under water. People began to return to their homes to begin the miserable task of getting rid of the smell and silt. No official records were kept during this period, but it is known that the floodwater was so high above Over Causeway that a barge sailed over it!

Though there were no records kept during the eighteenth century of the severity of the different floods, one flood of that era is always recognised as being the worst. Perhaps not for the amount of water in the river, but for the damage it did.

The winter of 1795 was very severe with large amounts of snow on high ground along the course of the Severn, with the river frozen over for much of its length. Come the spring a rapid thaw set in, melting the snow and breaking open the ice on the river. As the river level rose the ice broke into massive chunks and flowed downstream with some speed. Many of the old bridges were destroyed as the ice swept into them, some built with timber were simply not able to withstand the forces of nature against them.

For Thomas Telford this great flood was a blessing. Telford was beginning to make his name as a bridge designer and today many of his bridges still grace the Severn. Over Bridge at Gloucester has even been preserved as a monument, a great tribute to one of the finest bridge designers. An even greater tribute was the naming of the new town of Telford in Shropshire after him.

During the early part of the nineteenth century a report was compiled on the navigation of the Severn. It was noted in 1816 that in several places the rocky beds that crossed the river impeded the passage of vessels. One solution tabled was to narrow the width of the river to

A Regent tanker barge carefully negotiates the flooded Worcester Bridge at Worcester.

raise the level, but there were concerns that flood water would not run off freely.

By 1841 the Severn was becoming hard to navigate even at Worcester. A narrowboat loaded with 24 metric tons of cargo and having less than 4ft of draught could not get over the shoals below the city.

Several meetings took place to decide how best to overcome this problem and finally it was decided to build a series of weirs between Gloucester and Stourport to raise the level of the river. River engineer Mr Cubitt was against the idea of fixed weirs and would have preferred to have had opening gates, shut in times of drought and opened to the bottom when the river was flooded. The fixed weirs are still in place today, but many would like to see them removed and replaced with compensating ones, as Mr Cubitt recommended!

November 1852 – The Great Flood

As the residents of the Westgate area of Gloucester awoke on the morning of Saturday 20 November they found their kitchens and cellars under several inches of water. Along the quay, St Mary's Square, St Catherine Street and Lower Westgate Street, all had placed boards against the exterior doors and filled crevices with clay. Furniture was floating in ground floor rooms; even animals were taken to the safety of the upper floors.

By the end of the day even the city gas works was submerged by floodwater, giving cause for concern as the fires in the retorts were extinguished. The company had no choice but to be very sparing of the supply to the city not affected by the floods.

Workmen at the docks were busily employed in saving the grain from the warehouses, moving it to the upper storeys as the local fire engine pumped water out of the vaults. This was ineffective, for however fast they could pump it out, as soon as they stopped, it would flow in again! Those warehouses located near to the Severn suffered the worst, with most of their stock ruined and only fit for animal feed.

By Sunday the level of the flood was still rising, with the only form of communication being by boat. Those who had decided to stay in their property in the upper floors of the houses suffered great misery as they were without any form of heating.

By Monday 2 November the flood reached its peak with a mark being recorded at Gloucester Lock of 22ft 7in above the sill. For safety reasons a note was issued stating that the supply of gas would be discontinued until further notice. Along the quay the water was up to 8ft deep, in many cases nearly to the top of the doors.

The level of the River Severn at Gloucester was 3ft above the level of the Gloucester & Sharpness Ship Canal and stop gates were in place at the lock to prevent river water from entering the canal. However river water did find its way into the canal by way of a culvert down by the timber ponds. Much to the annoyance of Mr Essie, owner of the timber yard, he found timber floating in his yard and was unable to operate the steam saw as that was fast becoming surrounded by water. An employee was sent to open up the sluice valves in an adjoining brook, which helped in taking some of the water away.

Even though the river was well above normal level and still in flood, a boat left the docks on the Wednesday bound for Worcester. The barge was laden with 40 metric tons of corn, some timber and other items when it suddenly capsized in a stiff breeze and the strong current soon sank the vessel. Luckily the crew were able to make it to the bank safely in a small boat.

The floodwater had also risen 18in above the railway line to South Wales and it was a curious scene when a steam locomotive came hurtling along the line and into the water. The water was scattered either side of the engine in a heavy spray!

March 1947 – Our Worst Flood

It had rained most days from the end of September 1946 until the middle of January 1947. This was followed by severe freezing conditions for two months making the ground frozen hard. From the middle of January through to the March over a metre of snow fell along the course of the Severn.

Then the rains returned, draining across the still frozen land into the river. What began as a slow thaw suddenly developed into a rapid one, with the snow melting with the continuous fall of rain.

The emergency began at Gloucester on Wednesday 19 March 1947 when senior officers from the council would hold regular meetings at the Guildhall. On that first day five monitoring posts had been set up along the Severn to check the rise, but by the following day three had been abandoned.

During the day only large lorries and small boats were able to move around the flooded areas of Gloucester. The army drafted in soldiers with more lorries to assist with the evacuation of people from their homes. Food was cooked at the local Calton Road School and

Severn in flood at Worcester, August 1912

Previous page: *Duck boards and rowing boats help everyone move around in a flooded Worcester street, August 1912*

distributed to those who needed hot meals. Hospitals were used to give shelter to many residents who had been evacuated from their homes; it was estimated that several hundred people had been made homeless.

450 homes were flooded, but the electricity supply was never cut off. Water did get into the gas main, which caused it to fail, requiring candles, matches and lamps to be taken to those homes that relied on gas for lighting. Extra coal was delivered to those who required it for cooking and heating. Fortunately the mains water supply was maintained, even though Mythe Waterworks at Tewkesbury was surrounded by floodwater.

A week later the floodwater began to recede and every house was inspected to check on what repairs were required. Extra police were drafted in to keep an eye on empty properties to stop thieves breaking in. Help was given to clean and dry out the houses, plus soap and disinfectant was issued to every property.

This 1947 flood still remains as the highest recorded since records began.

Chapter Eight
Mysterious Disappearances

Bridges over rivers are a great attraction to those who want to end their lives, people who have reached the depths of despair and simply cannot cope with the problems racing around inside their heads. Suicide, a harsh, simple word for something so tragic, leaving family and friends in great pain, always wondering if there was something they could have done to prevent their loved one taking their own live.

Some bridges gain notoriety for being popular with people who wish to end their lives. Bristol's Clifton Suspension Bridge, spanning the Avon Gorge, is one such bridge. Since it was built in the mid-nineteenth century, many hundreds of distressed people have jumped off the bridge, some landing in the river, some in the mud and others caught on the rocks on the cliff side. Many means have been implemented to try to stop people from committing suicide from the bridge; high wire fencing along the walkway, even a telephone hot line to the local Samaritans.

The Severn has never reached this notoriety but many people have, and continue to, end their lives by jumping off the many bridges that cross the river. The Severn is notorious though, for adding to the list of missing persons, for the bodies of a lot of people who jump into the river are never found! This creates a mystery that is rarely solved, questions which remain unanswered, such as did the person take their own life? Did they fall in the river by accident? Or are they still alive with a new identity?

The winter of 1995 was what can only be described as giving most people the 'winter blues', long periods of rain, grey skies and for those living close to the Severn the misery of more floods. Within a matter of four weeks three people mysteriously vanished, all leaving their cars in isolated spots, two never to be found again.

5 January 1995 – Gloucester

As the new year of 1995 dawned the River Severn was rising steadily until, on Tuesday 3 January, the waters topped the banks to run over the A417 road as it dipped from the large roundabout at Over, Gloucester, down towards the village of Maisemore. Then suddenly, on the following day, temperatures plummeted and the county was gripped by a big freeze with flooded roads now becoming dangerous as motor vehicles slid on the ice.

Despite this cold snap the Severn continued to rise, peaking on Thursday 5 January, the day that one Gloucester housewife was last seen alive. June Kennedy (43) had arranged to meet her husband Ted on that day at 10.15 p.m. in the Tailors House, a popular public house in Westgate Street, Gloucester. She never turned up and was reported as a missing person to the police.

The tug Speedwell *stuck across the Severn outside of Gloucester Lock. The grain barge* Tirley *went to her assistance, but she too became stuck.*

The following afternoon at 2.45 p.m. police found her red Vauxhall Nova car abandoned in Llanthony Road, Gloucester, close to the derelict Llanthony Priory, an area close to Gloucester Docks and not too far from the Severn. The police helicopter was brought in to carry out a search from the air, whilst tracker dogs were used on the ground.

Then on the Saturday, less than forty-eight hours after June had been reported as missing, a body was found floating with debris in the River Severn at Arlingham. Shortly after 1.00 p.m. a rescue crew from SARA brought the body ashore, later to be identified as June Kennedy.

16 January 1995 – Tewkesbury

The Severn remained on flood alert, all river traffic unable to navigate upstream of Gloucester. An unusual sight was the grain barge *Tirley* lying in Gloucester Lock, fully laden with her 250 metric ton cargo of wheat, waiting for the floods to subside so she could continue her journey to the flour mill at Tewkesbury. Normally vessels are not allowed to moor in the lock, but this week Gloucester Docks was being used as a film set and the sight of the *Tirley* in camera shot would have spoiled the theme of the film!

Her sister vessel the *Chaceley* and the *Tirley* were the only two commercial carrying vessels still operating on the River Severn. Working between the Sharpness and Allied Mills flour mill at Tewkesbury these barges desperately fought to keep the river alive, a losing battle, though, for in 1998 they were once again laid up at the mill, where today they still lie.

The family of thirty-four-year-old Angela Bradley became concerned when, two days after she was last seen, her white Citroen AX car was found abandoned near to Mythe Bridge at Tewkesbury. Angela had last been seen alive at 9.30 p.m. on Monday 16 January as she drove her fiancé from their home at Tuffley to his place of work in Brunswick Square, Gloucester.

Police and members of SARA carried out a search of the Severn for twenty miles downstream of Mythe Bridge, hampered by the floods and the spring tides running that week. The local press issued a description of Angela: 5ft 6in tall, proportionate build, short, dark curly hair and a sallow complexion. She had been wearing a dark blue tracksuit top, light blue trousers, pink socks and black boots.

Come Monday 23 January the police had stopped searching along the banks of the Severn as the floods were making it difficult and dangerous. On 27 January police issued a statement to say that despite their intensive search of the surrounding area and along the Severn, there had been no sign of Angela Bradley.

Gloucestershire continued to be lashed by rain and gales, with the Severn remaining high and on flood alert for most of this period. When eventually the grain barge *Tirley* was able to leave Gloucester Lock both crewmen kept a keen eye out for any signs of the missing Gloucester woman. It is not unknown for bodies to be left in fields on the bank and caught up in trees as flood levels recede, but nothing was seen. To this day the body of Angela Bradley has never been found.

Mythe Bridge at Tewkesbury.

1 February 1995 – Richey Edwards

Towns and cities throughout the UK have buskers entertaining the public as they rush by, many ignoring the poor soul with their hat collecting money as they either sing or play an instrument. Some try both, though not all, are successful, sometimes singing out of tune to the annoyance of everyone who has to suffer it! Now some authorities are even holding a form of audition and if you are lucky enough to pass then you will be issued with a pass, which will give you permission to perform in that town.

Cardiff did not hold such auditions in 1984, which proved to be good news for one James Dean Bradfield, who would stand in the shopping arcades with his cheap acoustic guitar belting out his version of 'Garageland'. A passer-by actually put money into his hat, to the somewhat surprised Bradfield, who allegedly began screaming at the generous hearted soul. 'What are you boyo, some kind of manic street preacher?' retorted the shocked shopper.

Like them or loathe them, the Manic Street Preachers became a big hit with their fans; four lads from the small Welsh town of Blackwood who, in those early days, struggled with their punk identity. They travelled all over Britain, never playing to more than fifty people, once playing to only two persons, and this in a club in Cardiff! Yet they persevered and finally in 1990 managed to secure a contract with a respected management company, to become the famed group they are today. With appearances at the legendary Glastonbury festival and at Reading they began to gain a reputation as having a hate towards other musicians and audiences alike.

Richey Edwards was born in 1968 and grew up in Blackwood with the other members of the group. Edwards had a good education, gaining three 'A' grades in his A level exams before beginning a history degree course at Swansea University. From those early Manic Street Preacher gigs the band began to sort themselves out as to who was to do what in the group, with Richey now on rhythm guitar and as lead singer, and Nicky Wire on bass, both these men also writing the lyrics to their songs.

Richey was not at peace with himself, with a darker side emerging from his personality.

Richey Edwards of the Manic Street Preachers.

He had a big interest in history and politics, fascinated by Ireland's hunger-strikers, including Bobby Sands who died from self-starvation in 1981. Richey Edwards at twenty-two years of age only weighed six stone and was turning to drink, stress taking its toll on this young man. Wire and Edwards had great plans for the group; to make a classic album and then split, an idea scoffed at by journalists. Following a show at Norwich, Richey was having a heated discussion with a local reporter when he calmly carved 4REAL in his arm with a razor, his way of expressing himself as meaning business.

Whilst performing on stage at a club in Bangkok, Edwards removed his shirt to expose his chest, full of lacerations made from a knife given to him by a fan! It was about this time that the Manic Street Preachers released their third album, The *Holy Bible* and shortly after this Edwards admitted to requiring psychiatric help and was admitted first to an NHS hospital before being treated at a private clinic. Richey later spoke of the treatment he had received for alcoholism, self-mutilation and anorexia. It was late January 1995 when he gave his last interview, a disturbed-looking figure, dressed in a pair of striped pyjamas, wearing them as a suit and sporting a closely shaved head; he spoke of his newly found sobriety. He was worried about not being able to have a lasting adult relationship and to quote in his words, 'Of course I would love to love somebody seriously, but I feel nobody would want to live with me.'

On Wednesday 1 February 1995 Richey Edwards walked out of the Embassy Hotel in Bayswater, London, and disappeared, but it was to be two weeks before he was reported missing by other members of the Manic Street Preachers. Later on Friday 17 February 1995 his silver Vauxhall Cavalier car was reported abandoned in the car park at Aust Services, close to the Severn Bridge. The car park attendant believed that the car had only been there for a few days. It was thought that at the time of his disappearance he was carrying no money or possessions and his passport was found in his flat in Cardiff.

Music magazine *Melody Maker* was inundated with correspondence from fans who were so distressed that many were saying they were cutting themselves and sending in photos of bleeding limbs. The magazine was so concerned that it contacted the Samaritans for advice on how they should react to this.

Richey Edwards, soon before he disappeared.

Even three and half years later reports would filter through that Richey Edwards had been seen. One such report came from a young lady working in the Canary Islands who thought she had seen him in a small Corralejo pub called the Underground Bar. One of the customers was so convinced it was him that they shouted, 'You're Richey from the Manic Street Preachers.' The man ran towards the door and fled, vanishing somewhere into the surrounding district.

Another sighting was on the Indian beach resort of Goa, where a college lecturer was sure he saw Richey Edwards with a group of hippies getting onto a local bus.

Richey is still classed officially as a missing person as the police have never closed the file. His family are desperate to know what really happened and why his car was abandoned at Aust Services, so keen for any news that may shed light on this mystery that they have contacted many agencies. The Coastguard, National Rivers Authority (now the Environment Agency), Maritime & Coastguard Agency, Gloucestershire Police, even the Hydrographic Office who supplied detail of tides for that date, were all helpful as to their theories of what could possibly happen to a person once they have jumped from the bridge.

His mother, Sherry Edwards, has never given up hope of finding him alive and has written this open letter to him:

> *To see you walk through our door or even hear your voice again would make me the happiest person in the world.*
> *I can never give up hope that you will return one day and wherever you are, I hope the pain you carried inside you has gone away.*
> *You are my precious son and I will never give up looking for you.*

Another car had been found abandoned on Saturday 31 December 1994 on the Severn Bridge with its engine still running. It was assumed then that the driver had jumped off the bridge into the Severn, but after an intensive search using lifeboats and helicopters, nothing was found. Through the car's registration number the owner was established, but it was not that of Richey.

Richey Edwards' abandoned car found at Aust Services.

The M48 Severn Suspension Bridge.

It was interesting to note comments made by the various agencies on the nature of the waters of the Severn in answer to Rachel Edwards' questions regarding her brother's disappearance:

It is recognised that a person jumping from the Severn Bridge at low water would become embedded in the mud, in which case the body would most likely sink into it and never be seen again.

If the body should be washed down into the Bristol Channel it is very unlikely that it would be taken out into the Atlantic, as the incoming currents are stronger and faster than those flowing down the estuary. It takes a long time before estuary water is 'flushed' out into the Atlantic!

However the movement of water within the estuary is very complex, having to cope with the second highest rise and fall of tide in the world and the vast amount of silt moved each day with the tides. This sediment could very easily submerge and hide a body forever.

Chapter Nine
The Battle of Tewkesbury

The fifteenth century: a complicated era of Kings, Queens and Dukes all battling it out to win supreme power, at times fleeing to the continent until safe to return to the shores of Britain. The era of the Plantagenet Kings, soon to come to an end with the death of Richard III in 1485. For 300 years the three related families of Anjou, York and Lancaster had provided fourteen monarchs to rule our island and shores across the English Channel.

The Wars of the Roses saw the House of Lancaster fighting with the House of York, not because of the dynastic struggle between both families, but because of the shortcomings of the young King of England. King Henry VI, a Lancastrian, was young, with little control of his subjects, making England an unpleasant place to live in, with a breakdown in law and order. The Duke of York made it known that he could sort this out, his priority being not to depose the King, but to restore law and order and to have control of the Government.

The River Severn was to have a major influence in the outcome of one of the major battles of the war. Not many bridges crossed the river, thus what few there were proved to be very important in moving armies of men between England and Wales. Although the Severn was quite shallow in places with numerous fords to enable men and animals to walk across the river, this could still be dangerous, especially with the fortnightly spring tide racing up towards Tewkesbury.

It has to be understood that the Wars of the Roses was not one long continuous battle, in fact there were only three major battles in the thirty-two years between 1455 and 1487, with fighting taking place in a total of about thirteen weeks. The first major battle took place at Mortimer's Cross, Towton, on Sunday 29 March 1461 when King Edward IV defeated a Lancastrian army led by Queen Margaret of Anjou. A year earlier, in 1460, King Edward's father, the Duke of York, had been killed at Wakefield.

After Towton there lasted eight years of peace, which ended when the Earl of Warwick began to assert his influence over the reigning monarch. Henry VI, the Lancastrian king, took the throne with Edward IV fleeing to the safety of Burgundy with his younger brother, Richard, Duke of Gloucester. Edward did not remain in exile long and with his brother-in-law, the Duke of Burgundy, returned to England in the March of 1471 to travel the length of the country in a bid to raise an army. He marched into London during early April and had Henry VI imprisoned in the Tower. He then travelled with his army to Barnet where on Easter Sunday on 14 April they defeated the Earl of Warwick.

Margaret of Anjou was born on 23 March 1429, the second daughter of Rene, Duke of Anjou. It was deemed that she should marry Henry VI in 1445 at Titchfield Abbey, Hampshire, followed by her Coronation at Westminster Abbey on 30 May. Immediately trouble began to flare up with the Queen favouring the Dukes of Suffolk and Somerset, with the three of them dominating the feeble-minded King Henry VI. The hatred of the French

King Henry VI

Margaret of Anjou, died 1482 (drawing of a stained glass portrait once in the church of the Cordeliers, Angers)

Margaret of Anjou

woman grew, the Government was incompetent and corrupt and there were many murders of prominent people, including the Duke of Suffolk in 1450.

It was inevitable that war would break out and when it did, in 1455, Margaret of Anjou assumed control and led the Lancastrian army into a series of violent battles, trapping and slaughtering men who supported the House of York. Her good fortune was short-lived and following a defeat at the hands of the Yorkists, she fled via Scotland to France, where she remained in exile for ten years.

As King Edward IV defeated and killed the Earl of Warwick at Barnet, Margaret of Anjou was landing on English shores at Weymouth. With her was her son Edward, Prince of Wales, his wife, Anne Neville, youngest daughter of the Earl of Warwick, and a small number of troops. The following day, while resting at the Abbey of Cerne, she learned from the Duke of Somerset of the death of the Earl of Warwick. The news devastated her and her first reaction was to flee England and return again back to France. She was persuaded to stay and to gather a large army to fight Edward IV.

Supporters of Margaret were sent to the West Country to recruit men for her army. Why men should wish to join her to fight remains a mystery, as in these hard times food was short and the thought of marching across rugged terrain must have been daunting! But recruit they did, finding many men who were willing to risk their lives in fighting for Queen Margaret. The army assembled, they then marched to Exeter to rendezvous with Margaret and her son before beginning the slow march to Taunton and on to Bath.

King Edward IV heard the news of Margaret's assembled army with alarm and decided to act quickly to raise a new army, having only recently disbanded one. Within three days he had formed a good army of artillerymen and made his headquarters at Windsor. He wished to commence battle with Margaret's army at the earliest opportunity, but was not sure of which route her army would take. She could march to London, along the coast to Kent or even cross the River Severn and head into Wales. In Wales one Jasper Tudor was himself assembling an army to march north to Cheshire and Lancashire and, if Margaret's Lancastrian army were to join his men, this would prove a formidable force for Henry IV to contend with.

Margaret's men reached Bath on Monday 29 April and learnt that Edward IV had re-formed his army and was keen to commence battle soon. To throw him off the scent she sent small groups of men to various parts of England, some to Salisbury, others to Yeovil, giving the impression that her army was advancing towards London. Her plan, though, was to cross the Severn at Gloucester and join forces with Jasper Tudor.

Edward IV could not be fooled for long and by 1 May he was at Malmesbury with the intention of stopping Margaret from proceeding north to Gloucester and thence across the Severn. From Bath her army had to proceed to Bristol to collect supplies of cannon, food, money and more men. It was here that she learnt of Edward's increasing proximity and cunningly sent a small band of men to Sodbury Hill to convince him that was to be the place of battle.

Edward sent his troops there as Margaret quickly continued her march towards Gloucester, soon joined by her men, who had fooled the King at Sodbury Hill. As King Edward IV realised that he was alone at Sodbury Hill with his army, he ordered scouts to search for the Lancastrian army but, surprisingly, nothing was found until 3.00 on the morning of Thursday 2 May. He then learnt that the opposing army was somewhere on the road between Berkeley and Gloucester. Edward also knew that she could cross the Severn at its lowest point by bridge at Gloucester, or by the shallow area at Lower Lode below Tewkesbury. If he acted quickly he knew that he could get a messenger to Gloucester to order the Governor, Sir Richard Beauchamp, to stop Margaret and her army from entering the city to cross the bridge.

Margaret and her army were relieved to arrive at the city gates at 10.00 a.m. on 3 May, having been on the march since midnight. Knowing that Edward was getting closer, Margaret did not want to waste time in forcing an entry through the gates, although she knew that many of her friends at Gloucester would have been willing to help her. She did make verbal threats to the Governor, who refused to be intimidated and refused to surrender. This refusal threw Margaret's plans into disarray for now she could not join Jasper Tudor and his army as they waited to march north to Cheshire.

Weary, the army had no choice but to continue their march the extra thirteen miles to Tewkesbury, where they arrived at 4.00 p.m. that afternoon. Her army had been marching for thirty hours, covering some fifty miles with only one short rest. The men were exhausted: foot weary, hungry, as food was short, and thirsty from lack of water to drink. The terrain they had marched through had been cruel, stony ground making it hard on their feet and then into woods, tiring as the men cut their way through bracken. No wonder then that Margaret's Generals decided that on their arrival at Tewkesbury the army could march no further and would have to make camp in the field they found themselves in that afternoon.

At 5.00 a.m. on the morning of 3 May King Edward, having realised he had been duped, gathered his army together and began the march north to Tewkesbury. His was a different terrain in which to march, no woods, but the open stony countryside of the Cotswolds. As with the Lancastrian army, food and water was short, made worse by the heat of a warm day and no cover to escape the sun. It is written that his army only passed through one stream that day and by the time they had marched through this it was turned into a muddy bog. Not very appealing to the King, who was travelling at the rear of the army in one of his carriages.

They arrived at Cheltenham, then just a small village, at about 5.00 p.m. that day and began to make camp when news reached him that Margaret was making camp at Tewkesbury. The King's men were weary, but realising that the Lancastrian force was making preparation for battle on the banks of the Severn, he knew that he would have to keeping marching towards Tewkesbury. With only a little food and water left, this was shared out amongst the troops before marching onto Tredington, a village three miles from where Margaret had made camp.

4 May 1471 – The Battle of Tewkesbury

Exhausted from their long march of the previous day, Margaret's men awoke on the morning of 4 May 1471 to face battle with the army of King Edward IV. Camped between the two rivers of Severn and Avon, it was a relief to have a supply of water in which to refresh themselves, though for some the Severn would be their last resting-place!

The field in which the Lancastrian force were preparing for battle was located close to Tewkesbury Abbey, surrounded by hedges and deep dykes, a good point from which to defend themselves. No one is absolutely sure of the precise field in which the battle took place, but it must have been near the present Gupshill Manor, where close by is a field known

King Edward IV

as 'Bloody Meadow'. This area would normally have been an excellent place in which to fight a battle, especially for the defending army, which the Lancastrians were. But they were tired and had only arrived there the previous afternoon, with no time in which to prepare the land to make the best defence, only time to place what wagons they had to their best use. Hopes were also dashed of any hope of men from Jasper Tudor's army crossing the Severn at Lower Lode to fight alongside Margaret's men.

6,000 men from the Lancastrian army faced 5,000 of the Yorkist foot soldiers, archers and horsemen, nervous as the time had arrived for which they had been recruited; to fight for either the King or Queen, with many losing their lives before the day was finished. A scribe had been riding with King Edward IV for some time and it is his account from which records describe how the day progressed. To put the soldiers in the mood for fighting, the day began with an archery contest, but ended in ruthless, bloody, hand-to-hand fighting.

Early that morning King Edward and his men broke camp and headed to where Margaret waited with her men (or rather they waited without her). It is said that she had left them and watched the battle from the tower of Tewkesbury Abbey. Her army was divided into three divisions, the right wing commanded by the Duke of Somerset, the left wing by the Earl of Devonshire and the centre by Queen Margaret's son, Prince Edward of Lancaster. In overall command of the army was Edmund Beaufort, the Duke of Somerset. King Edward also arranged his army in a similar manner, with Richard, Duke of Gloucester; William, Lord Hastings, and George, Duke of Clarence (King Edward's brother), together with the King, all leading their own division of men.

Richard, Duke of Gloucester

On arriving at the field of battle, instead of mounting a charge, Edward decided to play a defensive game, provoking his enemy with a bombardment of arrows and shot. This harassment caused the Lancastrians to make some rash moves, one being the Duke of Somerset leading his men into a charge against the guns of the Yorkist in a bid to silence them. With Somerset and his men alone in amongst Edward's army they were soon forced back to where they had charged from. Pursued by The Duke of Gloucester, the men broke ranks and fled towards the Severn, jumping into the river to escape more bloodshed, the water now running red with their blood.

King Edward took advantage of the situation and quickly advanced into the Lancastrian area. The battle became bloodier and fiercer with many of the commanders killed in the fighting, amongst them the Earl of Devonshire. Prince Edward himself was mortally wounded, crying out as he fled towards the town for the Duke of Clarence to help him before he died. The remaining Lancastrian army split up, with soldiers fleeing to both rivers to escape the bloodshed, others escaping into the countryside. Some took refuge in surrounding churches and the Abbey itself, that was until Edward appeared at the doors with his men and slaughtered the Lancastrians inside. A local priest had tried to prevent the King from carrying out such a terrible deed in that House of God, but nothing could have stopped Edward from entering. Such was the outcry of this terrible deed that no services were held in the Abbey for a month and then only after the Bishop of Worcester had re-consecrated it.

Edward IV and his army were the victors and to show his appreciation to his men he had forty-three of them knighted. Not so fortunate were some from the Lancastrian army!

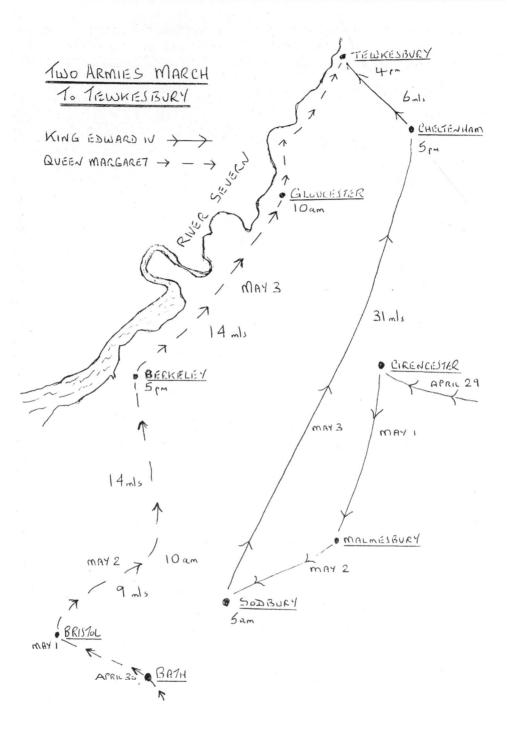

Plan of the route taken to Tewkesbury by the two armies.

Two days after the battle the Duke of Somerset, Sir John Langstrother, and other men of distinction were removed from the Abbey to be brought for trial before the Duke of Gloucester and Duke of Norfolk. They were all found guilty as traitors and sentenced to be executed that very day.

There was to be no rest for King Edward IV as he heard that support was growing in the north for the Lancastrians and in Kent also. News was soon brought to him that his own men had defeated both these armies, so Edward set off to march into London in triumph.

What of Margaret of Anjou? On hearing of the defeat of her army at Tewkesbury she left the town and crossed the Severn at Lower Lode and sought refuge at a house in the nearby village of Bushley. She later moved towards Worcester, stopping, it is believed, in Little Malvern Priory on Sunday 5 May.

Whilst resting at Coventry between 11 and 14 May Edward heard that Margaret had been discovered at Malvern and ordered that she be brought before him. On 21 May King Edward IV entered the City of London, with Margaret and her ladies-in-waiting having to endure being part of the triumphant procession. That same day it was learned that King Henry VI, Margaret's husband, had died in the Tower of London.

Later that day Margaret was also imprisoned in the Tower, where she remained for a number of years until Louis XI of France paid a ransom to secure her release. She then left our shores and returned to her native France, to end the final eleven years of her life in peace before dying in poverty in 1482.

Few who travel along the Severn at Lower Lode today realize the amount of blood that was spilt into the river from men slaughtered in the nearby field from the Battle of Tewkesbury in 1471. More blood was to be spilled into the Severn from battles fought during the Civil War in the seventeenth century, but that is another story.

Chapter Ten
Severn Railway Tunnel

Before the railways came, the Severn carried most of the cargoes being transported around the country. Then life became faster and people wanted their goods the following day, not in several weeks! The great web of rail track that wove around the British Isles eventually terminated in London, but the most direct route between the capital and Wales had one stumbling block, the River Severn. Below Gloucester, where the river becomes an estuary, the Severn is wide with large sandbanks exposed at low water. Where the long second Severn Crossing Bridge now dominates the skyline is an area known as English Stones with sand beds replaced by rock.

At high water the full width of the estuary is covered by water, not so at low water though, for one and three quarter miles across the river at the English Stones the riverbed is dry, as water rapidly flows through the deep rocky channel known as The Shoots. In 1645 men from King Charles' Royalist army fled across the Severn from here into Wales, closely followed by Cromwell's troops. The tide was ebbing fast as Cromwell's men crossed over the English Stones in the local ferryboat, only to be suddenly left high and dry on top of the rocks. The ferryman convinced them that they could walk ashore from here, but the tide turned and as it came racing back it swept them all away to their death. Cromwell was so angry that he gave orders for the ferry to be shut down; it reopened again in 1718 as the New Passage Ferry (the other ferry operating between Aust and Beachley was known as the Old Passage Ferry).

The railway companies realised the benefit of linking their lines in as short a possible route between the thriving cities of Bristol and Cardiff. To overcome the difficulties of crossing the Severn Estuary, a long pier was built on the Welsh side of the river at Portskewett with a similar pier being constructed on the English side. A broad gauge line ran eleven miles from Bristol, via Horfield, then through a tunnel at Patchway, near Bristol, down to the Severn opposite Portskewett. This service was opened in 1864, but it soon became apparent that freight could not be carried, and this at a time when the Welsh coal mines were beginning to increase production as more new pits were being opened. The only other alternative was the tortuous route via Gloucester, circuitous with steep gradients and adding sixty miles to the journey.

Pressure was put on the railway companies to provide a better crossing of the Severn, the most obvious way being a bridge as tunnelling was still in its infancy, full of risks and uncertainties. One bridge design was of a two and a half mile viaduct, over 100ft above the water, with three openings. With the cost estimated at £1,800,000 it was considered far too expensive and a possible danger to shipping. A man with twenty-five years of tunnelling experience, Charles Richardson, presented his plans for a tunnel under the Severn at a cost of only £750,000. With none of the risks associated with a bridge the Great Western Railway began to show interest in Richardson's plans, but first he had to convince and gain support from John Hawkshaw, the railway company's chief engineer.

The entrance to the Severn Railway Tunnel.

When built it would become Britain's longest railway tunnel, four and a half miles beneath the Severn Estuary, so no wonder the Great Western Railway didn't readily accept Richardson's plans. Hawkshaw saw no problems with Richardson's plans, indeed he had already discussed the practicality of building a tunnel under the English Channel. Another formidable character that had to be convinced about building the Severn Railway Tunnel was the chairman of Great Western himself, that fine railway engineer Sir Daniel Gooch. However, Parliament finally passed Richardson's plans in August 1872 and the building of the first shaft began on 22 March 1873 at Portskewett.

Before work began on the tunnel, the railway company had built six cottages and an office on land at Portskewett, close to Sudbrook Farm. Then a single-track railway line was laid into the village to bring in supplies of bricks, timber and other materials required for the work ahead. A Bristol company had been awarded the contract to sink the first shaft, 15ft in diameter and 200ft deep, but four months after starting they had only dug to a depth of 60ft. Two large springs were then opened up which meant more large pumps had to be brought in to take away the excess water. It was not until December 1874 that they reached the required depth of 200ft and a heading 7ft square could be started towards The Shoots.

Men worked in difficult conditions night and day on twelve-hour shifts, hand drilling the rock as well as blasting, but still they were only progressing 12ft each week! During January 1875, in a hope to increase the rate of progress, air compressors were installed on the surface to drive power tools at the face. This was not popular with the men, until they had to return to hand-tools when the air compressor broke down! Now using power tools and with the introduction of working three eight-hour shifts they were progressing at the rate of 50ft per day.

To further disillusion the men working underground, they soon learnt that construction had begun on the Severn Railway Bridge across the Severn from Sharpness to Lydney. July came and the heading was 300ft long under the river, but becoming more difficult as they hit more fresh water behind the rock. Richardson became concerned about this and built a 6ft thick wall, about 340 yards from the shaft, incorporating a heavy iron door complete with valve to enable the heading to be sealed off in the event of flooding from the fresh water springs.

By August 1877, two and a half years after work first began on the tunnel, the men had dug a heading nearly a mile long. To drain the tunnel of the large amount of fresh water coming from the springs it had been necessary to bore a second shaft alongside the original. Great Western now thought it time to award contracts to other companies for the completion of the tunnel, but were horrified at the amount estimated by those who tendered for the work, sums between £987,000 and £1,350,000 were received! It was the uncertainty of problems that these companies may find which forced them into making such high bids. In the event Sir John Hawkshaw persuaded his company that a bid from Thomas Walker should be accepted. Both men had worked together on Brunel's tunnel under London Docks and on the London Underground. However Charles Richardson advised Great Western that no contract should be awarded until the heading had been cut for the full length of the tunnel.

Therefore a couple of new, small contracts were awarded to local companies to sink a shaft on the Gloucestershire side, to be called the Sea Wall Shaft, and two shafts in Monmouthshire known as Marsh Shaft and Hill Shaft. From these shafts other headings were dug, providing the 1 in 100 gradient of the tunnel and also to provide a drainage area for any water that may be encountered. Work was progressing well and with powerful pumps installed any water found was soon taken away.

Two years later in the October of 1879 only 500ft separated the heading from the original Old Shaft in Monmouthshire and the Sea Wall Shaft in Gloucestershire. During these two years, work had been progressing steadily without too many problems, but all that was soon to end. Unknown to the tunnellers a huge amount of spring water lay trapped behind rock that they were about to cut into.

In what can only be described as terrible conditions, the men toiled long and hard as they cut into the rock, working in noisy, dark and wet surroundings. Long hours were spent breathing in dust as the rock was cut away from the face of the tunnel. Suddenly, on Thursday 16 October, a great gush of water cascaded from the face sending the men running as fast as they could back towards the Old Shaft. It is reckoned that because the men were on a change of shift no lives were lost; even so their only way of escaping this great flood of water was through the second Iron Shaft. In an attempt to stem the flow of water into the workings balks of timber were placed across the heading, even so this did little to stop the Great Spring pouring in at an estimated rate of 360,000 gallons an hour. Within twenty-four hours the tunnel was completely flooded!

The day following this disaster, Great Western chairman, Sir Daniel Gooch, was several miles upstream at the new Severn Railway Bridge to attend the ceremony of seeing the last bolt tightened on the bridge. Unaware of the flood he was casually inviting important guests to walk with him through the tunnel, saying to them that they may get a little wet!

It was time for Great Western directors to act and appoint an official team to take charge of operations at the tunnel. Sir John Hawkshaw was appointed as Chief Engineer, but he would only accept this position on the understanding that Thomas Walker was the main contractor and Charles Richardson was to act in an advisory capacity.

Thomas Walker did not arrive at Portskewett until December, by which time the site had mostly been abandoned. The majority of the men had left to look for work elsewhere, not an encouraging sight to greet someone who had been brought in to get the tunnel completed. All workings underground had been suspended with only a couple of pumps still in use. Before beginning work in the tunnel again the water had to be removed and then prevented from flooding the workings a second time. Thus Walker spent his first six months on site constructing two large engine houses with a large pump in each to take away the spring water.

Meanwhile Richardson had devised a method of sealing off the spring at the rock face. Oak timbers shaped to the contours of the tunnel were to be wedged in place, albeit under 140ft of water. Divers wearing heavy suits and helmets were employed to carry out this difficult and dangerous task and to take some of the pressure off them the pumps were restarted. As was to be expected, considering that they had not been run for some time, they soon broke down.

By July 1880 the large pumps at Sudbrook were installed and ready for use and in only eight hours the water level had been reduced by a few feet. But without warning one pump blew apart sending bits of metal everywhere, narrowly missing the divers. All their good work was wasted and as the tide raced in the workings were fully flooded again. It was not until 14 October that the pumps were working again.

With the water level reduced it was noticed that a large amount of fresh water was still entering the workings. Then it dawned on them that someone had not shut tight an iron door built into the timber dam, which should have been preventing spring water entering the tunnel. A diver by the name of Alexander Lambert was sent to walk the 1,000ft from the Iron Shaft, dragging his cumbersome air hose behind him, in an attempt to close the door, all in total darkness. Two other divers assisted Lambert, making sure the air hose did not become detached from him. Sadly Alexander Lambert could not complete the task, his air hose was floating against the roof of the tunnel and due to the amount of debris in his way it was impossible to get within 100ft of the timber dam. It was even more hazardous as Lambert made his way back to the shaft with his air hose becoming wrapped around timber supports and abandoned debris and skips.

Thomas Walker had heard tales of a Wiltshire man, Henry Fleuss, who had been experimenting with self-contained underwater diving suits. He was invited to Portskewett to give a demonstration of the suit, although it had only been tried out to a depth of 18ft. With Lambert in his conventional diving suit trailing an air hose behind him, Fleuss donned his suit and both men attempted to walk through the tunnel. It soon became apparent that Fleuss was not a diver and after three attempts both men had to return to the surface.

Not to miss a chance of getting the vital valve closed, Lambert was asked to don the self-contained diving suit and see if he could walk along the tunnel himself. Walker warned Lambert to take care as his life depended on that one small oxygen tank on his back and once down in the tunnel he would be alone and in terrible danger.

As Alexander Lambert vanished down the shaft and into the flooded tunnel men on the surface waited nervously, every minute seeming a lifetime, talking quietly amongst themselves, wondering how he was progressing. Suddenly, an hour and a half later, Lambert reappeared, jubilant and excited as he had managed to get to the iron door and close the valve. Not only was Lambert's task to close the valve on the iron door, but he had also to pull away two iron rails, and unfortunately he had only managed to remove one. Although willing to go back down again and have another go, there was no spare oxygen for him to use; Fleuss would have to go to London to bring back more supplies.

Lambert did manage, on Fleuss's return, to go back into the tunnel and remove the offending rail. The pumps were got to work again at full power, but it would still take another two months to get the level down at the face to a depth of 2ft. Now James Richard, a foreman from the pumping station, was able to walk to the face to make a check on the state of the wooden dam. He was surprised to see water pouring through the iron valve. Then he realised that Lambert had been turning the valve the wrong way; instead of closing it down he had in fact fully opened the valve! Not really his fault, the valve had a left-hand thread and in darkness he would not have realised this.

On Monday 13 December miners foreman, Joseph Talbot, opened the iron door within the dam to see how safe it would be for tunnel engineers to walk through to assess what damage the flood had created. The following day engineers did walk the length of the tunnel and decided to brick off the Great Spring in a hope that it would not give any more problems.

No progress was made in tunnelling during 1880 due to all efforts being used to shut out the Great Spring, but work did continue on the surface. More houses had been built for the construction workers, indeed, even a mission hall to house 250 people. Now into a new year, workers and bosses alike were hopeful that tunnelling would progress without more disruption.

The first problem of the year was to be the weather on the surface; snow and frost. Because the tunnel was so close to the coal mines in the Forest of Dean, stocks of coal to feed the boiler were kept to a minimum, but when snow fell on 18 January to a depth of 4ft, they soon ran out! The company was so desperate to keep the pumps working that workers were sent around the area buying and begging whatever amounts of coal they could find. After the snow came frost, which then prevented men from working on projects up on the surface. Not a very good start to the year.

On 9 May 1881 Thomas Walker ordered the door through the headwall, that had been closed for five months, to be opened. They found ahead of them much debris and, worse, the roof had fallen in about one and a half miles from the Old Shaft. Conditions were bad down there, with men having to push skips loaded with timber for an hour through the debris to get to the damaged roof with the task of repairing it. Working in dust and dirt, Walker gave orders that the men were not to waste time in returning to the surface to take their meal break, but to eat their food underground, and to stay there for ten hours! Tempers became short, with Walker's men suffering taunts from other workers, resulting in fights and then the men going on strike.

Walker was not sympathetic to their cause, telling them to either get back to work or collect what money was owing to them and catch the 2.00 p.m. train from the nearby station. They caught the train, which in some respect pleased Thomas Walker, as with the workers went the troublemakers. Was it coincidence or an accident due to the current hot, dry spell of weather, for on the following day the wooden pier at Portskewett serving the New Passage ferry burnt down? The strikers were blamed for starting the fire, something Walker would did not believe, defending them to the hilt. By the end of the week many of the strikers had drifted back to work to begin once again working ten-hour shifts underground to restore the roof and clear out all the debris.

It has to be remembered that the heading bored beneath the river is only a 7-9 sq.ft narrow tunnel, simply to link Monmouthshire with Gloucestershire. Having achieved this link, the tunnel would have normally been opened up to its full working size with a team of men cutting and removing material from the sides and top. Up until the flood from the Great Spring, 150 yards of rock prevented the heading between both counties from being completed. Before linking the two headings Walker decided to open them up to their full size, hoping that this would prevent further flooding from the spring water. All went well until about 600ft from the Sea Wall Shaft, when water began pouring in, not fresh water though, but seawater cascading down from the roof.

Above them in the estuary there was a tidal pool, which at low water was estimated to have a depth of only 3ft. Walker's men walked out at low water to check the level of Salmon Pool, but could find no leak. So thirty men were ordered to link arms and to walk out into the pool waist deep in water. Suddenly one of them vanished! The leak had been found. Pumps were stopped to allow the tunnel to flood, whilst a schooner laden with bagged and loose clay dumped her cargo into the pool. How right Walker was not to have opened up the remaining 150 yards of headings between the two tunnels, for this prevented the whole of the tunnel system from becoming flooded.

The two headings were eventually linked on Monday 26 September 1881 to give better ventilation for those men working in cutting out the tunnel to its full size. As explosives were used to cut the face of the rock, conditions would have been quite unbearable through lack of air. It is surprising that no serious accidents were recorded at this time, although one foreman, Joseph Talbot, was injured as a charge blew out and hit him in the face. At the end of 1881 500ft of the tunnel had been cut to its full size, no distance when realised that when finished it was to be 23,000ft in length.

A civil engineering project of this size could not be completed without a serious accident, especially in the nineteenth century when the term 'Health & Safety' was unheard of. Considering the conditions the tunnellers worked in and the problems associated with the flooding from the Great Spring, one would have expected to hear of many men losing their lives. Yet it was not until 1883 that the first serious accident occurred, resulting in loss of life. It was 1.00 a.m. on 9 February as men were finishing their shift and preparing to return to the surface in one of the winding cages. Labourer John Nash was at the surface handling skips from the tunnel, which were full of clay when, with his mind not fully on the job, he pushed an empty skip into the shaft. The skip fell 140ft onto the cage full of miners, killing three of them, before bouncing on into more miners who were stood around waiting for the next empty cage. Another man was killed with two others seriously injured.

Work continued well in the construction of the tunnel, with Sir John Hawkshaw reporting that nearly one and a half miles had been completed. At last it looked as though the worst was over and now the men could look forward to a completion date. However, their hopes were dashed yet again when another disaster took place on 10 October. Men were working in the heading running from the Sudbrook shaft when suddenly a massive volume of water burst in to the workings and picked up the miners and equipment to sweep them into a completed part of the tunnel. They tried, but it was impossible to walk back through the water to assess what had caused this sudden inrush. There was no loss of human life, but three horses stabled in the tunnel were drowned.

This catastrophe was bad enough, with the pumps unable to keep up with the level of water increasing all the time from the Great Spring. Worse was the weather forecast for the next twelve hours; gales, rain and an exceptionally high tide. Seventy men were down in the tunnel on the early evening shift aware of the weather forecast, but not of the predicted high tide. In darkness at about 7.00 p.m. the storm arrived quickly, followed by a tidal wave that swept over the land with a leading wave of at least 6ft. People ran for safety grabbing their children and heading for higher ground, the fires of the boilers that fed the pumps were extinguished and water poured down the 100ft Marsh Shaft. The men below ran for their lives, first hoping to escape by being brought to the surface in the cage, but this was out of action due to the storm. A few of them did try to climb the ladder up the shaft, only to be forced back by the force of water coming down. Thinking fast, the men realised that if they ran along the tunnel they would soon be climbing the steep gradient as it rose out into Monmouthshire. As they ran, they came across a wooden platform that was in use to repair part of the roof, but would this be enough to save them?

Men on the surface were very worried about their colleagues below and in a desperate attempt to save them lowered a rowing boat down the shaft and into the tunnel. Below, the men had not gone far along the tunnel when they found their way blocked by fallen timber which necessitated them returning to the shaft for a saw. Back at the obstruction with the saw one of them dropped it into the murky water and had to return to the shaft once again for another saw! Remarkably, all eighty-three men were eventually rescued from the platform.

The flooding in the tunnel was worse now than when the Great Spring burst through for the first time in 1879 and it was time for Thomas Walker to deal with the problem once and for all. Three new pumps were ordered which put Walker further over budget, already £100,000 in the red. The spring itself was diverted along another new heading to be pumped to the surface through a 12in cast iron pipe.

By the autumn of 1885 the tunnel was almost completed and Sir Daniel Gooch, on 5 September, invited guests to travel in a passenger train hauled by an engine from the Great Western Railway through this fine civil engineering project. After six years work on the tunnel Walker thought it time for a break and sailed away to Buenos Aires to price up a job for the construction of a new dock. However all was not well in the tunnel when water pressure behind an area of brickwork began to blow bricks away from the wall. Walker was ordered to return home immediately in a telegram sent by Sir John Hawkshaw, but it was another couple of months before he arrived back in Britain. The pressure behind the brickwork was reduced and a decision made to build a permanent pumphouse to take away water from the Great Spring.

The great day finally arrived; on Wednesday 1 September 1886 the tunnel was opened, first to freight trains only, then two months later passenger traffic was allowed through. With a length of four and a quarter miles below the Severn Estuary it was claimed to be the longest railway tunnel in Britain, taking thirteen years to build and carrying the Paddington-to-South Wales main line of the Western Region. It is a credit to those brave men who risked their lives to complete the tunnel that over one hundred years later it is still in use, much as it was on the day it opened.

One hundred years after the tunnel was opened, the second Severn Crossing Bridge was carrying traffic between England and Wales. Officially opened by HRH Prince Charles, Prince of Wales, on Wednesday 5 June 1996, it is Britain's longest river crossing with the road carried on thirty-seven columns and a section spanning the shipping channel through The Shoots. At a final cost of £333,000,000 the site once employed 1,000 workers at its peak in 1993. Following the completion of the Channel Tunnel this construction site was claimed to be the largest in Europe.

The first bridge support in the estuary on the Gloucestershire side rests on rock above the Severn Railway Tunnel, carefully placed to avoid damage to the Victorian tunnel. Construction of the bridge only took four years to complete and with today's modern Health & Safety Act very few accidents occurred.

Before it opened the claim from the authorities was that the bridge would never be closed to traffic, unlike the Severn Suspension Bridge sited a little way up the estuary crossing the river between Aust and Beachley. In times of strong gale force winds this bridge is regularly closed to traffic. Yet within a few weeks of the Second Severn Crossing Bridge being opened to traffic it closed! Not because of strong gale force winds or a major road accident, but because of smoke. One lunchtime, a large chemical fire developed at Avonmouth and with the prevailing winds, large volumes of acrid smoke drifted up the estuary. Because of the possible danger to drivers and their passengers it was considered necessary to close the bridge.

The bridge can be seen by all, admired and credited as a fine piece of civil engineering, but what of the tunnel? Crossing the river some distance beneath ground few people get to see it, even the portals at the tunnel entrance are not that easy to see, but during its life millions of people have passed through it and, with good fortune, so will many more.

Chapter Eleven
The Haw Bridge Torso Mystery

With the many murders committed in Gloucestershire, none has captured the imagination more than the one committed in 1938, still referred to as the 'Haw Bridge Torso Mystery'. Officially still listed as unsolved, many thousands of words have been writtenon it, a newspaper was sued for libel over it and even a film has been made of the story.

Haw Bridge is located in the village of Tirley, midway between Gloucester and Tewkesbury. Built in 1825 to replace the ferry which had crossed the Severn here for many centuries, the bridge was to suffer serious damages in 1958 following a collision by a tanker barge coming downstream whilst the river was in flood.

Monday 10 January 1938

While out walking, Hubert Charles Price of Tirley crossed Haw Bridge and noticed blood-stains on the parapet. At first he attached no importance to this, but on arriving home he decided to inform the local police. He sat down to write a note, which he planned to hand to the passing bus driver with instructions to hand it to PC Knight at the neighbouring village of Corse. Having written the note he had a change of heart and decided instead to telephone PC Knight to report his discovery.

Left: *Hubert Price who discovered bloodstains on Haw Bridge.*

Right: *248 Old Bath Road, Cheltenham, home of Captain William Butt and his wife Edith.*

After receiving the call at 1.00 p.m. PC Knight visited Haw Bridge, took note of what he saw and reported this to senior officers. Dr E.N. Davey, a Gloucester Royal Infirmary pathologist, was assigned to carry out exhaustive tests on the blood and two days later was to report his findings to the police.

Meanwhile the police made a thorough search of the surrounding area and found a brown button with threads of tweed fabric attached. Some distance away they also found what appeared to be a belt thought to have come from a girl's coat. On the bridge parapet fragments of bone and flesh were also found! House to house enquiries were made to ascertain whether anyone had seen or heard a car knocking someone down. Laundries were asked to assist after the police had found a chamois glove with bloodstains on it and a tag with the letters CLR614 written inside.

A local couple from Apperley, Mr Belcher and his wife, said that they had both been awoken by the noise of a car coughing and spluttering late on the night in question.

On Wednesday 12 January at 6.00 p.m. Dr E.N. Davey took his findings to Gloucester Police Station. Together with Chief Superintendent A.J. Wayman, Davey came to the conclusion that the blood had come from an animal. It was quite feasible that a passing motorist had struck a sheep and then thrown the dead animal into the Severn from the bridge.

Monday 24 January 1938

Mrs Irene Sullivan was a nurse-companion to the wife of retired army captain, Capt. William Bernard Butt, at 248 Old Bath Road, Cheltenham. Her home was at Tower Lodge, an impressive building on the hill out of Cheltenham above Leckhampton. Her twenty-seven-year-old son Brian worked in London as a professional dance partner, earning considerable amounts of money accompanying ladies on the dance floor. He could be happy and charming, but otherwise often became very moody. Being an only child (an older sister had died when he was about four years old), and having lost his father when only three months old, there developed a strong bond between him and his mother.

When Sullivan was young the family moved from London to Dowdeswell, near Cheltenham. He left school at fifteen to work in a motorcycle showroom in Bath Street. During this time he would regularly be seen at the Town Hall dances, then a year later left for London to frequent dance halls in the city. As a professional dance partner he came into contact with fashionable young ladies. During regular weekend visits back to Tower Lodge he would bring home young ladies from this circle. Rumours had it that these girls were pregnant and came to Cheltenham for abortions, performed by Mrs Sullivan, who was an untrained nurse.

One place he frequented quite often was the Piccadilly Hotel and it was here that Capt. Butt was also noticed visiting on several occasions. Although people in London knew little of Brian's private life they did learn of his marriage on Saturday 4 April 1936 to thirty-two-year-old Miss Mary Margaret Edwards of 24 Tottenham Court Road, London. Sadly this marriage was to only last a few short months with both of them separating to go their different ways. Finally Brian left London in late 1937 telling everyone he was going to Cornwall.

Brian Sullivan had come home for the Christmas of 1937 and had spent an enjoyable time with his mother. During their conversations he had told her that he would be returning to

Above: *Brian Sullivan, who was associated with the Haw Bridge Torso Mystery.*

Left: *Irene Sullivan, mother of Brian, and house-keeper to Mrs Edith Butt.*

London on 10 January to see his friend Keith Newman. Although Irene Sullivan visited Tower Lodge several times after Christmas she did not go in as the house was locked, but she had become suspicious on Monday 24 January.

She entered Tower Lodge and discovered twenty-seven-year-old Brian dead in his bedroom, dressed in his pyjamas, with all crevices in the room sealed and the gas turned on. A verdict of suicide was recorded at the inquest and he was buried in the southwest corner of Leckhampton churchyard.

Thursday 3 February 1938

Three local fishermen were out fishing on the Severn close to Haw Bridge when at about 7.30 a.m. they were shocked to see a torso of a man in their nets. Attached to the centre of the torso with twine were two white bricks. Immediately the trio of Jack Dudfield, Edgar Bevan (both from Tirley) and Sidney Church (of Apperley) rang the police and soon PCs Knight and Greenall were on the scene. It could be clearly seen that a saw had removed the missing limbs from the torso, with the legs having been cut off close to the hip joint and the head cut off close to the hollow of the neck. From the appearance of the torso it would seem that it had not been in the water for very long. The police thought the body was that of a person of a mature age, appearing to be that of a physically fit man. Later that day the torso was removed to Cheltenham Mortuary.

Police began dragging the river close to Haw Bridge on 5 February, hampered in their efforts to find the missing limbs by the state of the river. The Severn was running at a depth of 16ft, some 4ft above normal level. At about 2.00 p.m. a shout was raised and a man in a boat could be seen holding a drag net with a limb and brick attached! The police pathologist quickly took this gruesome find to a local cowshed for examination.

Further tests were carried out on the original bloodstains found on the bridge parapet some weeks before and now it was ascertained that they were from a human.

Following the sudden death of Brian Sullivan at Tower Lodge, police had searched the house and what they found alerted their suspicions to the mystery torso found in the river at Haw Bridge. Amongst his belongings was a set of car keys traced to a Daimler belonging to

Haw Bridge, scene of the torso discovery in 1938.

The three fishermen who discovered the torso in their nets. Left to right: Sidney Church, Edgar Bevan and twenty-four-year-old Herbert 'Jack' Dudfield. Ironically, Jack Dudfield was killed on 25 October 1960 whilst involved in the Severn Bridge disaster. He was mate on the Wastdale H *(see chapter 2).*

Thousands line the bank and Haw Bridge to see if any more human remains are found.

one Capt. William Butt. Letters were also found exposing the fact that Sullivan and Butt had been lovers. It was then noted that Butt had not been seen since 4 January.

News of this macabre find at Haw Bridge was making headlines in the local press and soon the crowds began to gather along the banks of the Severn at Tirley. On 10 February 10,000 people gathered there, causing traffic chaos. Traffic was held up for three miles either side of the bridge, with cars parked bumper to bumper for two miles. More people gathered outside Tower Lodge as police began digging in and around the house looking for clues. Interesting finds were twine and bricks matching those found on the torso, plus a freshly dug hole about 6ft deep and thought to have been prepared for the concealment of a body. Under the floor-boards police also found an overcoat belonging to William Butt with bloodstains on it and under the stairs a box concealing an axe with more blood on the blade.

The police had appealed to anyone who had information of the whereabouts of William Butt to come forward. From that appeal they received information that a man of Butt's description had left a Daimler saloon car registration number KV 4595 at Regent Motors Ltd of Regent Street, Cheltenham at 10.40 p.m. on 4 January. The car was sealed and several items from it were taken away for examination. The investigation intensified and a massive search was made at Leckhampton Quarries, Cranham Woods, Haw Bridge and Tewkesbury, with every vacant property within a fifteen-mile radius of Gloucester and Cheltenham searched.

On further investigations the police pieced together some strange facts: if a car had killed Butt, it was not Sullivan's; it was unlikely that Sullivan cut up the body, he was not strong, only nine stone and small, so there must have been a third man. Sullivan had been seen with a stranger, a large, moustached, older man in the Black Bear Hotel at Tewkesbury roundabout on 4 January. It was a fact that Brian Sullivan had died after the date the pathologist stated the blood stains found on Haw Bridge were animal and before the torso was discovered, but was it a fiction that Sullivan's death had been arranged to lead the police to believe that he had killed William Butt?

Captain William Butt whose torso was found in the River Severn at Haw Bridge.

Tower Lodge, Leckhampton, Cheltenham, home of Irene Sullivan and son Brian.

Back at Haw Bridge the crowds waiting to see if more human remains would be discovered were not to be disappointed. First an arm was dredged up, then a leg, followed by the second arm. The feet and hands had been severed from the limbs, also weighed down with white bricks. During the three weeks of dredging the head was never found. From all these finds it was ascertained that this was a male in his mid-fifties of 5ft 9in tall and weighing ten and a half stone. On one leg a scar was noted at the knee, which pointed to the description of Capt. William Butt, but without the head no certain identification was possible.

Capt. William Butt was a retired army officer aged fifty-two and had served with the Worcestershire Regiment in 1919. He was 5ft 9in tall, with tattoo marks on one arm, brown hair, which was turning grey, and had a full military style moustache. He was last seen in Cheltenham at 10.40 p.m. on Tuesday 4 January wearing a soft hat and light tweed suit.

On 10 January 1938 the torso was buried in an elm coffin in Cheltenham Cemetery with only one mourner attending, that of the keeper of the graveyard. The Revd S.W. Betts, curate of St Paul's Church, Cheltenham, conducted the short service.

At the inquest held in March 1938 into the mysterious death of the unknown person found in the Severn, the cause of death was thought to have been from excessive bruising in the lumbar region, suggesting that he had been hit from behind by a fast moving vehicle. The jury was unable to identify the dead man as William Butt, so Sullivan could not be implicated in the murder. The jury only took twenty minutes to return an open verdict, but before they had announced this the coroner, Mr J.D. Lane, stated to them that, 'There is no evidence as to the cause of death, and insufficient evidence to the identity of the body.'

Today, with DNA testing and the technical facilities in use by the police, there may have been a different outcome to this case. Meanwhile this will remain as one of our unsolved murder mysteries.

Chapter Twelve
Danger from the Air
The Second World War

Gloucestershire was to become an important area in the advance of the aircraft industry when in 1929 Sir Alan Cobham moved his Municipal Aerodrome Campaign to Brockworth, near Gloucester. With his de Havilland biplane he flew some 40,000 passengers around Britain, including schoolchildren, who he allowed to travel free! During the 1930s the threat of another war loomed and plans were being made to develop our air power.

But people still wanted fun and Sir Alan Cobham was there to provide it, in the form of his exciting air shows. The public was enthralled to see planes flying in formation, wing-walking and even bombing cars on the ground. No wonder that Cheltenham Borough Corporation refused him permission to stage such a show over the town. Not to be beaten he found a farm at Churchdown, a small village located midway between Cheltenham and Gloucester. His shows were the inspiration of future pilots, who would soon be recruited by the RAF to fight bravely in the inevitable Second World War.

Soon airfields were springing up in Gloucestershire, Brockworth, Filton (near Bristol, then part of the county), South Cerney, Kemble, Little Rissington and Moreton-in-the-Marsh. As the training of pilots commenced so did the accidents! Shoppers in the busy Cheltenham Promenade were surprised one Saturday to see a light aircraft suddenly appear out of the gloom and fly only a few feet above the ground, narrowly missing trees and buildings. It is thought the pilot had become disorientated. The last shoppers saw of him was him pulling his joystick back and flying off towards Prestbury. Others were not so lucky. One aircraft did crash into property in Cheltenham, demolishing a house, but thankfully the pilot had managed to bail out and landed safely in the back garden.

It was not until 17 October 1939 that the first German bomb was to fall in Britain, in the Orkneys in Scotland and six months later the first casualty fell victim to bombing, again in the Orkneys on 16 March 1940. Gloucestershire was not to receive the massive bombing raids as did the larger cities of London, Coventry, Bristol, etc., but certainly bombs were dropped on the county. Indeed Gloucester received its first hit by a bomb in September 1940 when a German bomb fell onto the house of Norman Bruton in Kenilworth Avenue.

Avonmouth Docks at the mouth of the Severn Estuary was a prime target for the enemy, easy to locate by bombers flying up the Bristol Channel during the month of September 1940. Heavily protected by anti-aircraft guns on the ground and Barrage Balloons tethered to the ground by steel cable, rogue aircraft would drop their bombs on whatever other targets they could find. Early one evening the Aust to Beachley ferry was attacked as it made its way across the estuary, fortunately escaping any damage or injury to passengers. Not so lucky was the village of Beachley two months later in November when a bomber came in low and dropped several bombs, then strafed the area with bullets, killing one person and injuring several more.

November 1940 was the beginning of the massive onslaught by German aircraft over Bristol, with eleven-hour raids, thousands of incendiary bombs dropped causing extensive damage to the city and surrounding areas, including Avonmouth Docks. The cold and snowy weather of January 1941 did not deter the enemy flying their raids and only added to the misery of those losing their homes on the ground. The enemy aircraft were not only dropping bombs but laying mines in the Bristol Channel also, creating an added danger to convoys which used to assemble here before beginning their dangerous voyage across the Atlantic.

Of course, whilst these raids were taking place, Britain was fighting back, but first airmen and ground crew alike had to be trained. Gloucestershire played a great part in this role with several RAF camps around the county used for this purpose. During the First World War there had been an operational airfield at Aston Down, so it was no surprise when it was reopened on 12 October 1938. Its main role in the war was as a fighter training unit with all the camaraderie that is associated with those brave wartime pilots.

Between 1940 and 1941 pilots of fighter planes would use the Severn Railway Bridge as a focal point to relieve their tension; many would fly between the two large spans on the Lydney side. The authorities were so concerned of the danger of this practice that a policeman was stationed on the lawn of the Severn Hotel to take note of the identification numbers of the aircraft. So many were reported that if every pilot had been court-martialled there would have been no pilots left to fight the war! Even an Anson was seen to fly under the bridge. It was not only the bridge that was used in this way, some aircraft were also seen to fly under the power cables at Newnham-on-Severn.

Soon it was quite common for pilots from Aston Down to 'buzz' the Severn Railway Bridge, which spanned the Severn between Sharpness and Lydney. Many came to grief as they attempted to fly beneath the bridge, as on 14 May 1942 when a Spitfire struck the water, recovered, but then crashed into a field about a mile from the river. By 1943 the authorities had had enough and three RAF pilots ended up on a court martial for endangering themselves and their aircraft in flying under the bridge. They were subsequently found guilty and reduced to the ranks.

Wartime Aircraft Lost in the Severn

21 October 1939
Gloster Gladiator from 262 Squadron crashed into the River Severn near to the Severn Railway Bridge. The pilot was saved.

20 December 1939
Bristol Beaufort L4468 from Bristol Flying School crashed into the River Severn. The pilot was killed; his body washed ashore at Avonmouth.

12 February 1941

Vickers Wellington T2855 from No.218 Squadron made a forced landing in the River Severn at Frampton. This airplane was returning from a raid on Bremen. The crew of six men were all saved.

22 February 1941

Heinkel He 111 German aircraft shot down from anti-aircraft fire at Portbury and subsequently came down into mud flats off Avonmouth. Of the crew of five, only one was saved.

19 June 1941

Bristol Blenheim L1471 from No.5 Operational Training Unit crashed into the River Severn off Lydney.

6 October 1941

Hawker Hurricane W9175 from No.50 Operational Training Unit crashed into the ground having been caught in the slipstream of another aircraft whilst flying in formation. It crashed near to the New Grounds at Slimbridge. The Australian pilot was saved.

22 October 1941

Hawker Hurricane W9263 from No.52 Operational Training Unit crashed into the Severn whilst flying low in the vicinity of the Severn Railway Bridge. The Canadian pilot was saved.

23 January 1942

Avro Anson N5324 from No.6 Operational Training Unit struck High Tension electricity cables in poor weather and crashed somewhere near to the River Severn. All crew were saved.

8 February 1942

Supermarine Spitfire R7135 from No.52 Operational Training Unit came down into Oldbury Sands in the River Severn. The Canadian pilot was killed and his body was washed ashore two months later.

24 April 1942

Supermarine Spitfire R7124 from No.53 Operational Training Unit came down into the River Severn at Newnham whilst flying low over the river.

14 May 1942

Supermarine Spitfire P8169 from No.52 Operational Training Unit had been flying in formation at 11.00 a.m. when it made contact with the water and carried on to fly under the Severn Railway Bridge. The aircraft finally came down in the Severn about two miles off Lydney. The Canadian pilot was saved.

23 July 1942

Supermarine Spitfire P7509 from No.52 Operational Training Unit crashed into the River Severn close to the entrance to the River Wye during firing practice. The pilot was killed.

30 August 1942
Miles Magister came down at New Grounds, Slimbridge. The crew of two were saved.

11 September 1942
Supermarine Spitfire P7676 from No.52 Operational Training Unit came down after striking the surface of the water. The Canadian pilot was killed.

13 January 1943
North American P-51 Mustang AL959 from No.170 Squadron crashed into the River Severn killing the pilot.

26 January 1943
Supermarine Spitfire P8207 from No.52 Operational Training Unit collided with another Spitfire from the same unit (Supermarine Spitfire P8208) and came down into the Severn. The pilot was killed. The other aircraft made a forced landing in a field on the shore; the pilot was saved.

23 August 1943
Armstrong Whitworth Whitley T4339 from No.42 Operational Training Unit crashed into the Severn killing all four crew members.

12 March 1945
Hawker Typhoon JR212 from No.55 Operational Training Unit crashed into the River Severn after taking part in a rocket-firing dive.

4 February 1954 – Turbo-Jet Britannia Crashes into Severn

A delegation from the Dutch airline KLM were on a visit to the vast Bristol Aircraft Co. works at Filton, near Bristol, to have a test flight on a new prototype Britannia aircraft. It was a chilly mid-morning as Britannia G-ALRX took to the skies with Capt. Bill Pegg, BAC chief test pilot, at the controls. All hopes were pinned on impressing the KLM delegation into seeing how magnificent this aircraft was and hopefully securing orders to supply the Dutch airline with a few.

An hour into the flight over Herefordshire things began to go wrong. One engine began to break up, with the turbine spinning out of control sending fragments of metal to the ground. Unfortunately some of the debris passed through the engine oil tank and caught fire. Eyewitnesses on the ground could clearly see the oil tank ablaze as Britannia G-ALRX passed over Ross-on-Wye, making the long sweep around before heading home. For nineteen minutes the fire raged as Capt. Bill Pegg headed back to Filton, but he realised he would not make it within only a few miles of the airfield, so instead he decided to land on the mud of the shores of the Severn Estuary near to Littleton-on-Severn.

Before bringing the stricken aircraft down into the mud Bill Pegg radioed Filton to say he was crash landing, followed by silence. Wreckage from the £800,000 Britannia was strewn

Britannia G-ALRX crashed into the mud of the Severn Estuary near to Littleton-on-Severn.

for 400 yards along the mud, but the wings remained attached to the fuselage and as they came to a stop it became covered in mud with the crew thinking they had gone under the water! Fortunately all thirteen men onboard escaped with only one suffering any injuries, but they still had to struggle through thick mud to the safety of the shore.

Engineers from Filton were quickly on the scene and in a bid to beat the next tide, which was due in five hours, steel hawsers were attached to the plane. Their plan was to winch the 67 ton aircraft off the mud, nature, however, was to beat them. A tug had left Avonmouth with a crane on board to assist in placing netting under the faulty engine so that it could be removed for inspection. Problems soon arose when it was discovered that the plane and engines were sticking in the mud! This is an area of the Severn where someone can be soon stuck up to their waist in mud if they are not careful.

Now it was the turn of the army to attempt to get the plane off the mud. They sent two tank transporters loaded with two tanks down the narrow lanes from the A38 at Thornbury. Once on the narrow lanes it became difficult to keep the transporter on the road due to patches of ice forming on the steep hill down towards the Severn. At one stage the tanks had to be taken off the transporters to enable them to negotiate a steep hill, with the tanks following on behind. The army had planned to use the tanks out on the mud to pull the plane to safety.

One final attempt was made to pull the plane off the mud on 6 February using a buoyancy tank and rubber floats fitted to the Britannia. This too proved to be unsuccessful so the aircraft was declared a total loss and was subsequently broken up on site. The Britannia had no insurance so the cost was borne by the Ministry of Supply. Some experts say the aircraft was a write-off due to misguided efforts in using nothing but steel cables to pull it off the mud.

Crash investigators at the scene of the crashed Britannia aircraft.

Crash investigators look for clues at to the accident at the crash site.

Britannia G-ALRX crashed into the mud of the Severn Estuary near to Littleton-on-Severn.

Following an inspection of the faulty engine it was discovered that a resonant vibration had been set up, which had swiftly eroded the gear teeth. Modifications were made to the new Proteus 3 engines and following intense testing no further problems were encountered.

There was, however, to be another crash involving a Britannia in the Bristol area. On 6 November 1957 Britannia G-ANCA was one hour and forty minutes into a test flight from Filton when, at about 1,500ft, it banked to begin a turn back to the airfield. Suddenly something was wrong with the aircraft and, as the Britannia began to lose height, Capt. Statham made a Mayday call.

Seconds later the Britannia banked in the opposite direction but, owing to the loss of height, struck the ground in a wood near to a residential area of Downend, near Bristol. All fifteen passengers and crew were killed but, although some houses were damaged, no one on the ground was killed. At the subsequent report into this accident, P.G. Tweedie, Chief Inspector of Accidents, stated his belief that the accident was the result of the aircraft developing a very steep descending turn to the right, which the pilot was unable to control. The reason for this could not be determined, but the possibility that it occurred as the result of autopilot malfunction cannot be dismissed.

Chapter Thirteen
Yet More Accidents

Saturday 1 February 1868

Both this and the following incident happened to staff and trains operated by Cambrian Railways, but that doesn't mean that this company was any better or worse than any other company operating in Britain at the time. Rail accidents occurred then as they do today, some could have been avoided, and some are just that, an accident.

During February of 1868 the River Severn was running exceptionally high, with abnormal floods affecting the upper region of the river. A single-track railway ran from Newtown to Caersws, following the course of the Severn and crossing the river by means of a wooden bridge.

A goods train comprising of steam engine and tender, trucks and a guard's van began to cross the Severn, when the flood water running across the track on the bridge swept away the train. The engine driver, Samuel Daniels, was found dead under the tender and his fireman, James Davies, was also killed, his body later found wedged between the steam engine and tender.

Wednesday 26 January 1921

This accident, for once, was not the fault of the dangerous River Severn, but was due to error by four railway workers at Abermule in Wales. The Cambrian Railway operated on a single track through this part, running parallel with the Severn from Newtown to Abermule. Being a single track, a complicated method of ensuring that two trains were not on the same line together had been devised. Quite simply something called a tablet was kept locked in a cabinet at either end of the single track and, when a train was due, was handed to the engine driver. This would operate a circuit-breaker at the other end of the track, thus locking the tablet in the cabinet so that it could not be removed and given to another engine driver.

Railway rules stated that only a signalman or stationmaster was authorized to handle these tablets, but at Abermule these were kept at the station and not in the signal box. Because of this, the rules had become lax and it was not unknown for two young station employees to handle the tablets.

On this day two trains were due to pass each other at Abermule at about 11.52 a.m., an express and a local passenger train. The signalman allowed the local train from Montgomery into his section and then left the station to return to the signalbox. Four minutes later, the bell rang at Abermule Station warning them that the Newtown express train was on its way, but there was only a seventeen-year-old lad left to deal with this. He released the tablet at the other end of the section, but failed to tell anyone that he had done so. Unknown to other staff, the express train entered the section at 11.59 a.m. as the local train was fast approaching from Montgomery. The local train arrived at Abermule and another employee collected the tablet from the engine driver and gave it to the relief stationmaster. The employee, who was a young fifteen-year-old lad with a speech impediment, confused the relief stationmaster somewhat, because without looking at the tablet it was handed back to the local engine crew.

The fireman accepted the tablet and put it in his pouch without checking it, then the station porter was ordered to tell the signalman to let the local train leave for Newtown. Unknown to the engine crew, they were in fact carrying a tablet for the Montgomery to Abermule section and speeding towards them was the express train carrying the correct tablet for the Newtown to Abermule section! To his horror, when the signalman returned to Abermule station, he could see what had happened and tried in vain to stop the local train. Too late, the crew of the express train saw coming towards them the local train, working hard up a gradient through a shallow cutting. The collision claimed the lives of fifteen passengers and the driver and fireman of the local train.

Sunday 8 August 1937 – Bank Holiday Weekend at Wainlodes

Before the days of motorways and fast cars, people from Gloucester and Cheltenham would flock to Wainlodes on a sunny Bank Holiday weekend to enjoy a good day out. This was Gloucestershire's equivalent of a seaside town, located about six miles out of Gloucester, upstream of the River Severn. With a large expanse of grass, a high red cliff and shingle beach, plus the Red Lion Public House, it was an ideal spot for the family.

This was a typical hot sunny Bank Holiday weekend and fifteen-year-old Harry Kingscott from Gloucester had gone on his bike to Wainlodes on his own to spend the day on the banks of the Severn. His parents had gone on a day trip to Porthcawl and on their return at 11.30 p.m. were concerned to find that their son was not at home. Knowing that Harry had been spending the day at Wainlodes, they decided to cycle there to look for him, without any luck. The following day his father rode to Cheltenham to ask friends there if they had seen him, but no one had.

The last person to see Harry was a neighbour, who said she had seen him at Wainlodes near the ice-cream van and later at 8.30 p.m., fully dressed and sat on the bank. Mr.Kingscott's son-in-law decided to go to Wainlodes on the Bank Holiday Monday to make a further search. He found Harry's cycle and, some distance away, his clothes.

During the following Wednesday, a crewman on a tanker barge shouted to coal merchant, Harry Young, as they passed Ashleworth that they had seen a body in the Water. Harry Young then took his boat out to the spot where the barge had reported the sighting and recovered the body of young Harry Kingscott. At the inquest held on Friday 13 August it was stated that Harry could not swim and the coroner recorded an open verdict.

The River Severn at Newnham-on-Sevem.

The Severn Bore. A frightening sight for anyone out on the river in a small boat.

1644, 1731 – Newnham-on-Severn

Along the 220-mile course of the River Severn, no place has received so many tragedies as Newnham-on-Severn. Although well documented in parish registers written by the local vicar, this was not unusual as most parishes did the same thing. Without these registers many facts of life may have been lost for good.

Death in the Severn at this popular village may have only received a few lines written in the register because life seemed very cheap then and didn't warrant much fuss, not as today when such stories make the headlines for days on end. Take for instance the drowning of seventeen soldiers in 1644 as they crossed the Severn in a boat, which was overturned by the strong-flowing tide. That is it! Nothing else to add, except to say that five of them are buried at Arlingham.

Ironically, in 1731 a Severn trow stuck on the sand near to Amity Crib, which resulted in seventeen passengers drowning, with a further four rescued by a small boat. Again, very little else was ever reported.

There must have been a reason why there have been so many tragedies here and perhaps the next story gives a clue.

Thursday 6 February 1809 – Newnham-on-Severn

Early in the morning, the ferryboat was swamped and sank in full view of people on both sides of the river, resulting in the death by drowning of the two boatmen, Thomas Knight and Thomas Rooke, and their passenger, a Mr Hewlett of Frampton-on-Severn. They had been coming across the Severn from Arlingham hoping to avoid the spring tide, when suddenly it arrived with a mighty bore wave heading it. To avoid being swamped the boatmen turned the ferry head-on to face the wave, but with such a powerful wave they stood no chance.

Tuesday 29 August 1848 – Newnham-on-Severn

Forty-year-old Revd John Lloyd Crawley, Vicar of Arlingham, had been returning from a trip to the Forest of Dean when he arrived at Newnham late that evening, only to find there was no ferry to take him back across the river. Impatiently, not bothering to wait for low water he foolishly set out to cross the Severn on horseback. With some fresh water flowing down he was soon knocked from the horse and drowned.

People became concerned when he didn't arrive home that evening and went in search of him. They were alarmed to find his horse near his home at Arlingham, which had a stirrup and stirrup leather missing. The ferryman said that due to the state of the Severn that evening he would not have taken anyone across the river, but made them wait until the following morning.

The Revd Crawley's body was found the following day a short distance below Newnham.

Monday 17 July 1889 – Newnham-on-Severn

A warm summer afternoon proved too tempting for schoolchildren from the local National School at Newnham. As the sun rose high in the sky during the early afternoon, the children frolicked with joy as they bathed and paddled in the shallow water about fifty yards from the shore. At about 1 p.m., seven-year-old Reginald Phillips slipped from the shallows into deeper water and his brother, nine-year-old Victor, seeing him in difficulty jumped in to assist him. Both vanished under the water and were never seen alive again.

Their father, Tom, was the local ferryman and was in fact returning across the river when he saw the commotion and hurried to the spot. He felt about under the water with a boat hook and soon recovered the body of the youngest lad. Then the tide began to race in so they had to abandon the search until later that afternoon when they were able to locate the body of his other missing son.

Wednesday 11 August 1937 – Newnham-on-Severn

Newnham-on-Sevem can look an attractive Severnside village, which of course it is, especially viewed from the opposite bank at Arlingham Passage with the early morning sun glinting across the river. But views can be deceptive, especially with a river as treacherous as the Severn. Here at Newnham, the Severn is tidal and at low water, with sandy-coloured mud flats showing above the water line, it looks very inviting to bathe in the water that meanders around them.

At the site of the old ferry crossing is an ideal picnic area and after collecting her daughter, Florence, from school Mrs Saunders thought she would treat her and let her play with her friends on the grass. Florence (10) had been tempted to paddle at the water's edge with other children when suddenly she and another young girl were swept off their feet by the strong current. Two young boys, Robin James (10) and Bernard Wheeler (13), had been playing in the ferry boat, which was anchored on a long chain, and heard their cries for help. They lifted up the anchor and went to their rescue and managed to pull their friend Elsie Parry aboard but as Florence was about to be dragged aboard, the boat swung around and she was lost.

Her mother, who lived in Windsor Cottage at Newnham-on-Severn, had been sitting on a seat above the ferry with her young baby, Philip, and saw it all happen. Later, three boat crews spent three hours dragging the river to try to find Florence, but could not recover her body until she was found a week later at Broadoak.

The headmaster, Mr W. Billings, wrote in Newnham School records for 11 August 1937:

Florence Saunders, pupil of this school, was drowned today at Newnham Ferry. Elsie Parry, her companion, was saved from drowning by Robin James, present pupil, and Bernard Wheeler, past pupil. The Coroner, Mr M. Carter, highly commended the gallantry of these two boys. The Headmaster had on many occasions warned the children of the dangers of the river: he had issued a special warning on the last day of term, 27th July.

These are only a few of the many tragedies that have occurred at Newnham-on-Severn over a vast number of years. A wander around the graveyard and a look in the church will reveal some more interesting facts.

1935 – A Sad Tale

This sad letter was forwarded to me whilst researching material for this book.

I am a Worcester man, [all my life], and I was intrigued by your letter in the evening paper. I am now seventy-three years of age and many years ago; [either 1935 or 1936], one of my boyhood friends lost his life in the River Severn.

Four of us lads, all about eleven to twelve years old, one by the name of Johnny Forsyth, went out one Sunday afternoon, [I believe Spring or Summer], on an expedition or adventure as we did in those days. We had made our way along the Severn, [our favourite haunt]; just north of Worcester to an area called Bevere to the large weir there. Young Johnny had gone a little ahead of us and down the concrete bank to the water edge, which was a rushing mind-boggling plume of water. He must have slipped on the wet edge, because in a second he was down and gone.

We thought we saw him come to the surface some way out, but that was all. We must have shouted and screamed because some person in a boat started looking for him out in the middle at the foot of the weir.

Unfortunately he was gone and we were left to tell his mother of this dreadful tragedy. I can still see young John in my mind eye, just as he was then, a happy carefree lad who always seemed to be laughing.

One day I shall go to my library and scan through the local paper of that time and find the reports about it. It will keep young John alive to me.

The other two lads with us were brothers, Sidney and John Allport. John is now deceased, but I still see Sid who is a little older than me.

I hope this is of some use, it will keep John Forsyth's name alive.

Yours sincerely

Geoff Hutchinson

I have left this sad tale just as it is without researching more into it. The thought of those three young lads losing their best friend and then having to go to his home to tell his mother that Johnny is missing, presumed drowned, must have been awful.

Sunday 4 November 1984 – Lydney Sands Drowning

It was a lovely, sunny Sunday afternoon, one of those nice winter days which are so tempting to go for a nice long walk. The Bedford family from Coleford had dropped off their eldest son, Richard (17), at a Lydney school where he was playing in a football match.

Their father, Robert, and mother, Hazel, then decided to drive on down to the harbour, where they parked their car near to the small dock. With their other son Scott (5) they then proceeded to walk out onto the sands, which with an afternoon sun glistening over them made it look an attractive proposition for a pleasant stroll. Conditions could not have been

Lydney Sands at low water level.

more perfect with the water around the sandbanks as still as a millpond. But the Bedford family had been lured into a sense of false security, not knowing how treacherous it can be to be out on the sands between tides.

They had walked out from the Lydney Yacht Club slipway onto Saniger Sands, which at low water looks like a thousand-acre beach. It is possible that they had gone out to view the remains of the wreck of the *Ramses II*, which had come to grief here on 23 March 1951. After reaching the wreck they continued to walk in the direction of Gloucester along the edge of the sandbank.

Unknown to them the tide had already begun to creep in; a small tide which, unfortunately, makes little noise as it runs over the sands. Not like a big tide, which can make a noise like an express train as it rushes in. Small tides are 'creeping tides' and Saniger's secret is that it becomes an island as the tide comes in. At this location, the tide rises by running in the wrong direction, pushing back downstream to link with the tide that has been running up the Forest shore.

At about 2.30 p.m. the Bedford family had been seen on the sands by William Higgs, a member of the Lydney Yacht Club. Knowing how dangerous it is to be out on Saniger Sands with the tide coming in he raised the alarm. Too late, the tide quickly covered the sands and there was no sign of the family.

A Naval helicopter from RAF Chivenor searched the area as did a lifeboat from the SARA unit from Beachley. Lydney Yacht Club also launched their rescue boat, but all three units failed to find any persons from the missing family. Thus at 7 p.m. it was decided to call off the search.

Friday 1 October 1982 – Workman Lost in the Severn

Local man, Fred Larkham of Westbury-on-Severn, had been contracted to extend a sewer pipe, which ran from Blakeney out into the river at Gatcombe. During the afternoon the river became quite turbulent with a strong ebb tide flowing, which began to make it difficult for Fred's men, working from one of his barges.

One of them, thirty-one-year-old Paul Sweetland, was working in a dinghy and, as he leant over the side to secure a rope to a buoy, the small boat began to drift away in the fast-flowing current. As a non-swimmer, Paul was reluctant to let go of the rope and soon ended up in the water, much to the horror of his colleagues. The strong current of the Severn was holding him below the surface and unless he let go there was a strong possibility of him drowning.

They shouted at him to let go of the rope he was holding as they could see he was being held under the water. Diver, Mike May, leapt into the water to assist Paul, but nearly became a casualty himself before being taken away by the ebb tide. He managed to swim to the bank and climb ashore to alert the police to the emergency situation. Fred Larkham himself dived in to try to save Paul Sweetland, but could not get him to let go of the rope he was so desperately holding.

Sadly Paul was swept away downstream with the fast-flowing ebbing tide and a call was put into the SARA Rescue Station at Beachley where their lifeboat, the *William Groves*, was launched. They searched an area from Beachley up to Berkeley Power Station without finding anything. A RAF helicopter from Chivenor, North Devon, backed up the search of the Severn near Gatcombe and downstream for a further five miles. But the chance of spotting a body in the muddy and choppy waters, together with frequent rain showers was slim. At 4 p.m. the search was reluctantly called off. To this day his body has never been found.

Paul Sweetland was married and had a six-year-old son, Neil, who now lives in Scotland and enjoys the time he is able to spend with his Uncle Keith reminiscing about the brothers' early days together. Both had joined the Merchant Navy on leaving school, but ironically, never sailed on the same ship together.

Tuesday 4 September 1990 – Severn Bridge Gantry Collapse

The Severn Suspension Bridge, which carries the M48 across the Severn between Beachley and Aust, was opened in 1966 and, as is the case with similar large structures, requires constant maintenance. On Tuesday 4 September 1990, there were eight gantries working under the decking of the bridge. The 35 tonne gantries were only two months old, suspended from the bridge by strong wire hawsers. In one of the cages three men worked on painting the underside of the decking, employed by HPC Coatings of Port Talbot.

Suddenly there was a loud bang and then the gantry gave way, plummeting onto the rocks below the Aust Tower before slipping into the fast-flowing estuary. Painter Mark Seaton (19) survived the 150ft drop from the bridge, but his colleague Robin Phelps (44) was killed. His body was recovered from the wreckage of the gantry two hours after the incident. A third man, Eric Sullivan (46), was also killed, presumed drowned in the river.

M48 Severn Suspension Bridge [See Chapter 8]

Mark Seaton was fully aware of what was happening as soon as he heard the loud bang with the gantry falling down to the river. On hitting the water he realised that he didn't have the strength to swim ashore against the strong current so lay on his back and floated. He could see his colleagues up on the bridge and even began shouting at them. Thirty minutes later a lifeboat from the SARA unit at Beachley rescued him, suffering from bruising and whiplash injuries.

Until after the inquiry, the other seven gantries had prohibition orders served on them by the Health & Safety Executive. One theory about the cause of the accident was that a cable from the gantry had snapped. The damaged gantry was later lifted from the bed of the river by air bags and towed to Sharpness for examination.

The Early Severn Estuary Ferry Service

Ferries were recorded as long ago as 1131 in use at Aust Cliff, better known as Old Passage. In 1802 the Union Post Coach would run a mail service every three days from Bristol using the Old Passage ferry through to Chepstow and Monmouth. Unfortunately disasters did occur with these ferries, with one such incident occurring on Friday 30 March 1855 when the ferry boat, *Despatch*, heavily laden with passengers and animals, sank in a squall. Seven people drowned.

As the railways became the better mode of transport, a new ferry service began in 1863 at New Passage, located a few miles down the estuary at Portskewett. The Bristol & South Wales Union Railway & Ferry operated the ferry and train, and passengers would be transferred from the train to the ferry on either side of the Severn.

With the dangerous tides and currents in this part of the Severn estuary, it was soon realized that the New Passage ferry could not operate for much longer. The opening of the Severn Tunnel in 1886 proved to be the end of the New Passage ferry.

The Old Passage ferry had also ceased to operate, but in 1920 Enoch Williams came to Beachley, saw the old ferry jetty and decided to begin a new car ferry service. This became the famous Aust-Beachley ferry, used by many motorists in its long history, including Royalty, until the opening of the Severn Bridge in 1966.

Now only one ferry remains in use on the Severn and it is located at Hampton Loade near Bridgnorth, Shropshire.

Ferry Disaster at Hampstall – 4 August 1919

Not all serious disasters happened on the Severn Estuary. One tragic event took place far inland, three miles below Stourport at Hampstall on the Bank Holiday Monday 4 August 1919. During that era, the River Severn between Gloucester and Stourport was full of pleasure boats, with crowds of visitors enjoying a day out on the river.

With no bridge between Stourport and Holt Fleet, the ferry across the river at Hampstall was in regular use, especially at weekends and Bank Holidays. The ferryboat was a small fishing punt and carried upwards of twelve passengers across the river, which was notably quite deep in this region.

Hampton Loade Ferry

George Jones had been the ferryman for one month only and on that Monday afternoon a large number of people arrived at the landing stage to cross the Severn. As the first nine got into the ferryboat he indicated that he was going to cast off, but was persuaded to take all seventeen passengers across together! Due to the overloading of the ferryboat the punt was firmly stuck in the mud, giving Jones problems in getting away from the landing stage, so someone used an old iron shovel to push them into deeper water.

As the men struggled to float the ferryboat, a cry went up that a pleasure boat was coming upstream and that the wash from her would assist in floating them. The *Arno* passed them and indeed did assist in getting the ferryboat afloat again, but now it was observed that there was only three inches of the punt above water.

As the ferryboat got into mid-stream they saw another steamer approaching them, this time it was the *May Queen* coming downstream from Stourport at quite a speed. All seventeen passengers in the ferryboat were standing as the steamer passed them and, as the boat lurched, one of the men in the punt fell backwards out into the river. Soon all the passengers had toppled out of the punt into the river and in their panic would have seen the *May Queen* carry on downstream without stopping. The only time the skipper of the pleasure steamer was aware that something was amiss was when he noticed all his passengers race to the stern.

Mrs Helen Greenhough of Astley Burf had counted fourteen people getting into the boat and shouted for the ferryman to stop taking any more on board. This was ignored so her husband, William, shouted to her to fetch their boat and give some assistance. As the ferryboat sank, Mrs Greenhaugh was able to assist in getting five people out of the water and into her boat.

Nine persons were drowned that afternoon and it wasn't until midday on Tuesday that all the bodies had been recovered from the river and taken to the Hampstall Inn. Later at the inquest, the coroner, Mr Brown, recorded a verdict of Accidentally Drowned on all nine persons lost. The coroner also called before him George Jones, the ferryman, and Joseph Meacham, who was in charge of the pleasure steamer. He sharply censured them, expressing the hope that what happened would be a warning to them for the rest of their lives.

The nine drowned were: Harry Matthews (40), Ethel Matthews (38) and Hilda Matthews (5), all of 86 Crockett's Lane, Smethwick.

Mrs Lydia Wilson (44) and her son, Joseph Wilson (9), of 85 Oliver Street, Nechells.

William Thomas Richard (40) and his son, Arthur Ernest Richard (5), of Carlton Road, Sparkhill.

Minnie Elizabeth Hyde (30) of 223 Brunswick Road, Sparkhill.

Mrs Elsie Ramsell (25) of 121 Middlemore Road, Smethwick.

Hampton Loade Ferry

Hampton Loade is located on the Severn, midway between Bewdley and Bridgnorth. Now it is a popular spot to view the private Severn Valley Steam Railway, as the powerful steam locomotives pause at the delightful station just a little way up the lane from the river. There has been a ferry here since records began, not as large as those that once plied the Severn Estuary, but simply a small pontoon pulled across the river by means of an overhead cable. Indeed, this is the only surviving ferry left on the River Severn!

Bill Parkes was the ferryman from 1942 until 1957 and this incident could well have been his last trip, as a submerged and waterlogged tree floating down river hit the ferry, which then broke free from the cable. Bill was left clinging to the short mast of his ferry as it began to fill with water and sail on down the Severn. By the time it had reached Arley he was up to his waist in water and now becoming concerned because of the failed attempts by others in boats to rescue him. At Arley the large ferry was sent out into the river in a successful attempt to pull Bill from his sinking boat. Eventually the Hampton Loade ferry was retrieved at Bewdley and taken back upriver to await its fate, as many thought it time a new ferry was introduced to this part of the Severn.

Look on a map of the Severn and many places will end with 'Lode' or 'Loade', usually these places will be located in a shallow part of the river, as the name comes from the Saxon word for ford. As bridges were expensive to build, the next best alternative is the ferry, thus why there were so many at work on the river. Many have tales to tell of accidents resulting in loss of life, such as happened at Hamstall, Coalport and Sandhurst.

In December 1964 an incident is recorded concerning the son of the ferryman, who operated the Hampton Loade ferry and lost his life when the overhead cable broke, which resulted in him drowning as the boat was swept downriver. Two sisters ran the ferry for many years afterwards, Mrs Kathy Evans and Mrs Annie James, who only recently retired to hand the service over to Darren Page.

Thursday 15 January 1885 – The Littleton Whale

The crew of a trow sailing up the Severn Estuary on a large spring tide were surprised to see the tail of a whale thrashing about above the water above English Stones. As the tide began to ebb, Isobel Durnell was in her kitchen cooking breakfast for her husband and was amazed to see the large whale beached at the mouth of Littleton Pill. The tide was running out fast, but the whale was still alive, although beginning to become feeble.

Local men from the village of Littleton-on-Severn held a meeting and decided that the next tide of that evening may carry the whale away from them and beach it at a different part of the coastline. Together, Jim and Moses White with George Sindry and his two traction engines hauled the whale ashore using massive chains.

Next day the village became famous with crowds of people travelling by train to Thombury, then walking the few remaining miles to the river to view the stranded whale. As soon as the whale had died, its mouth was prised open with a long stake and people were charged a small fee to stand inside. One man of 6ft in height said he was able to get into the whale's mouth and stand upright!

The whale was 68ft long, with a mouth 12ft wide when opened. It was claimed that 40,000 people came from far and wide to view this strange sight.

Soon the people of Littleton-on-Severn were tired of seeing the crowds flocking to the village, so the whale was towed away to Bristol, where again a price was charged to climb inside. The carcass then began to rot and was cut down for manure.

Today signs still point to Whale Wharf at Littleton-on-Severn, a reminder of how a sad event can soon be turned into an attraction by local entrepreneurs.

The large whale beached at Littleton-on-Severn in 1885

Epilogue

There is no conclusion. As long as the River Severn flows from the source to the sea there will be accidents resulting in people drowning. Lessons have been learnt and people are now more aware of the dangers from the river, which is no longer a popular place in which to swim, while Health & Safety rules ensure that workmen working on and near the Severn obey new laws.

No longer is the river used as a commercial waterway; if it were, the practice of racing up the estuary to be first at the swinging light would cease, two or three barges tying alongside one another as they sailed out of Sharpness empty would be forbidden and crewmen would certainly have to wear lifejackets as they worked on deck. Below Sharpness any commercial vessel navigating the Severn Estuary must have the services of an estuary pilot on board to ensure the ship arrives and departs safely. For an inward bound ship the pilot will board off Barry, South Wales, and stay with the vessel until it is moored in the sea lock at Sharpness. The pilots make the manoeuvre from the estuary, between the piers and into the basin, look easy, but none take it for granted, all respecting the river and not relaxing until the ship is moored in the lock.

Should the future be that commercial vessels were to once again use the River Severn above Gloucester for the transportation of goods, then new rules and regulations would have to be brought in. The last commercial carrying barges to travel the Severn between Gloucester and Tewkesbury were the two large grain barges operated by Allied Mills. Sadly these finished working in 1998 and still remain laid up at their mill at Tewkesbury. During the last days of their working life, there were few regulations in place as to how they operated on the river above Gloucester. The skipper required no tickets of competency; as it has been since vessels first appeared on the river. If the current master thought the mate was competent to become a skipper, then that was it! The main problem, suffered by the crew of these grain barges during this latter period, was the lack of maintenance carried out to the river. Overgrown trees hampered their passage up and down the notorious Parting above Gloucester. The regular spring tides depositing tons of silt onto the river bed in The Parting didn't help either, during the summer months the barge would be rubbing along this silt, at times the crew wishing their craft had wheels fitted to the underside of the hull!

Flooding is dreaded by those who choose to live alongside the Severn, a fact of life which will never go away, and why should it? For that is what nature designed rivers for, to take away excess water off the land during times of rain and as a safety valve built flood plains every so often to allow more water to spill over onto this land. Man in his greed of the last few hundred years has decided to build on these flood plains and now our newspapers are continually reporting people's worries and concerns as their property regularly becomes flooded. The cry is for more flood defences to be built, but enough is enough and remember, one man's flood defence is another man's flood. Those who choose to live alongside the river must also respect the river and accept that the river level will rise in times of heavy rain and snow.

But how many people does flooding kill? Very few compared with other types of accidents that occur in the course of a year on the river.

Swimming used to be common on the Severn, not just in the idyllic locations farther upstream, but even in the most dangerous section of the river at Sharpness. Of the numerous deaths at Newnham-on-Severn, many were the result of children playing in the river. Now this practice is frowned upon and unless we have an exceptionally hot spell, as was the case in 1995, few people will be seen swimming in the Severn. John Hinton from Worcester relates how in his day the Severn at Worcester was recognised as a place in which to swim:

> There were bathing barges moored in the river with water flowing through them, one for the ladies and the other for the men, to teach children how to swim in moving water. The instructor was William Brown, the first man to escape from a sunken submarine during the First World War. At the end of his working day he would make his way to the River Teme to give voluntary instruction to children, who gathered there to swim in the evenings.
>
> Of all the children that Brown taught none had been heard of drowning in the river, for his method was to teach survival rather than sport, to swim with the river, even though you may have to travel a greater distance to reach the bank. Another tip of his was that you did not jump into the river; with waterlogged tree trunks floating below the surface it would be very easy to suffer a serious injury.

Swimming and boats don't mix; John Hinton well remembers occasions when he would be swimming under water and hear the sound of a propeller approaching! It was a terrifying experience as he surfaced only 2ft away from the propellers and he vowed never to get into that situation again. But not all boats have engines and he relates how he surfaced one day to find himself between the hull and blades of a rowing eight, much to the consternation of the cox.

If there has to be fresh worry of potential accidents it may be from the growing sport of surfing the Severn. Increasingly surfers come from all around the world to surf the famous Severn Bore, indeed the world record for the longest surf is held by a Gloucester man who achieved this on the Severn in 1996. Dave Lawson managed to surf for a distance of 5.7 miles and thinks that it will be difficult to better this, although there are those who desperately want to! Dave lives on the banks of the Severn at Gloucester and respects the river more than most and is also worried about the danger of this practice. Whilst out surfing on a big tide, Dave can be seen in his distinctive pose on the board, closely followed by his stepson Mike May in a large inflatable craft, as a rescue boat in case any trouble should occur. Dave Lawson says the biggest fear is being thrown by the wave into the bank. The wave will roll you over and over at least a dozen times before letting go and during this time the body is bruised and battered from hitting the bank. The fear is being struck on the head by a rock or low hanging branch of a tree.

Finally, as these last few words are written, news has broken; in a tragic accident in Shrewsbury, two Shropshire schoolboys have died as the car they were travelling in plunged into the River Severn. One lad aged thirteen, the other only twelve, were killed as the car they were passengers in slid into the river at Sydney Avenue. The driver of the car was the older boy's brother, who managed to escape from the sinking car and raise the alarm.

In 1786 the Royal Humane Society was founded due to the high death rate of people killed in the River Severn. The year before, eight people lost their lives at Maisemore as they were returning home from a day out at Ashleworth fete. Then a few years later in 1799, twenty-eight workers from the local china works at Coalport lost their lives as the ferry they were on sank in the Severn.

Sadly it is inevitable that the River Severn will continue to claim lives.

The Severn is a powerful river and, despite man's best efforts, has always flooded almost on an annual basis somewhere along its length. Here, Worcester feels the brunt of a heavy flood in August 1912.

Bibliography

Roger Cowles, *The Making of the Severn Railway Tunnel*

Alan Earnshaw, *Trains In Trouble* (Penryn: Atlantic Transport)

P.W. Hammond, *The Battles of Barnet and Tewkesbury*, (Alan Sutton, 1990)

Ron Huxley, *The Rise and Fall of the Severn Bridge Railway 1872*, 1970 (Alan Sutton, 1984)

Christopher Jordan, *Severn Enterprise*

John Rennison, *Wings Over Gloucestershire* (Stroud: Aspect Publishing)

Tewkesbury Festival Committee, *Battle of Tewkesbury 4th May 1471*

Margaret Willis, *The Ferry Between Newnham And Arlingham* (Alan Sutton)